GRADES I TO

MW01182032

MEMORY BOOK

FOR LUTHERAN SCHOOLS

Published under the Auspices of
THE BOARD OF PARISH EDUCATION
The Lutheran Church — Missouri Synod

CONCORDIA PUBLISHING HOUSE · SAINT LOUIS

FOREWORD

$\equiv$ MEMORY WORK in religion has been part of the curriculum in Lutheran elementary schools since their organization. Because of spiritual ignorance among the people Martin Luther already in the year 1529 called upon the bishops, pastors, and preachers to adopt a fixed form of the Catechism and to inculcate it "word for word" on the young. In addition to the word memorization Luther emphasized the teaching of "the sense also, that they may know what it means." He declared that every Christian should know by memory a certain minimum of Christian fundamentals, or a brief summary of Christian doctrine, upon which "a richer and fuller knowledge" might be built. Luther himself had memorized not only the Catechism, but large portions of Scripture, and is said to have quoted Scripture largely from memory in his writings. In Lutheran schools today pupils memorize, as a rule, all of Luther's Small Catechism and selected hymn stanzas, Scripture passages, and prayers. Often a number of psalms are memorized in their entirety.

THE PLACE OF MEMORY WORK IN LUTHERAN SCHOOLS

The objectives of memory work, method of memorizing, manner of conducting the recitation, and procedures of evaluating outcomes have been extensively treated in the *General Course of Study for Lutheran Elementary Schools* (St. Louis: Concordia Publishing House, 1943, pp. 45—54) and need not be repeated here. The reader is referred to this source for a full discussion of the place of memory work in Lutheran schools. It will suffice here to state that, besides providing a solid foundation of Christian doctrine, religious memory selections serve Christians as a defense against temptation, comfort in sorrow, and reassurance in time of danger, and thus provide a source of spiritual strength at times when strength is most needed. Many pastors have testified that their ministrations are made easier among members who are fortified with a rich store of religious memory selections.

CONTENT OF MEMORY BOOK

In content, this memory course does not differ radically from older courses that have been published and used extensively, though it is based largely on the newer textbooks of religious instruction as they are listed later in the Foreword. Of the total of 703 Scripture passages in the 1943 synodical Catechism, 325 have been included. This number covers adequately the chief doctrines and life situations for which Christians need ready reference to Scripture. All of Luther's Small Catechism, including the Table of Duties and the Christian Questions, has been included. Hymns and prayers have been selected with a view toward supplying gems for important life situations, worship occasions, and the chief festivals of the Christian church year. A number of selected psalms have been added. Among the older courses consulted for content and grading of materials, *Graded*

Memory Material for Lutheran Schools, by Herman Voigt, deserves special mention. Grateful acknowledgment is herewith made of assistance obtained from this and other sources.

ORGANIZATION OF COURSE

The organization of the present course is entirely new. All materials have been arranged in logical units, and Bible passages, hymn stanzas, and prayers do not appear separately as in the typical older courses. Only the Catechism units have been kept separate, because it seemed advisable to preserve the proper sequence in memorizing the Chief Parts. New selections are introduced by appropriate statements intended to give meaning to the selections. Bible passages are numbered as in the Catechism, and the Scripture references are also listed. All selections in Grades I to IV and the hymns in all grades are printed out in full. Selections printed out in full are phrased or paragraphed to make learning easier. Reviews are frequent. At the beginning of each unit, selections of similar content memorized in previous grades are reviewed. Each grade reviews all the work of the three previous years. At the end of each year the current year's work is reviewed. In the seventh grade, the work of Grades I and II is reviewed in addition, and in the eighth grade, the work of Grades III and IV. The work for each grade is divided into 180 lessons to correspond with a nine-month school year.

The course listed for Grade VIII offers a number of alternatives. In schools of eight grades, it may be used in confirmation instruction; or it may be omitted entirely in favor of a thorough review of all materials memorized during the previous seven years. In schools of nine grades, the materials listed for Grade VIII may be used in confirmation instruction, and Grade IX may review all selections of the previous eight years; or if the pastor prefers to use a separate course in confirmation instruction, the course suggested for Grade VIII may be taught in Grade IX.

CORRELATION SCHEDULE

A correlation schedule is added to aid the teacher in providing for frequent practical and meaningful use of memorized materials. Its use is explained in the introduction to the schedule which appears in the Teacher's Edition.

PROVISIONS
FOR INDIVIDUAL DIFFERENCES

Generally speaking, this course represents a maximum of materials to be memorized. In order to provide for differences of individual schools and pupils, a number of selections which may be dropped without disturbing the unity of the course have been marked for possible omission. Asterisks are used to indicate these selections. Their number may be increased or decreased according to the needs of the class or the individual. A few Catechism selections may appear rather difficult for the grade to which they have been assigned. Reference is especially to Grade II, Lessons 42—49; 59—66, and Grade IV, Lessons 85—95; 141, 142, 144—147, which were included in these grades to keep the sequence of the Chief Parts. In some schools and in the case of certain pupils in every school it will be advisable to postpone the teaching of these materials to the next higher grade. The same applies to parts of the Table of Duties and the Christian Questions listed in Grades VI—VIII. In no case should memory work be made an undue burden for the child. A smaller amount of material well learned is preferable to a great amount half learned. In cases where the school year is shorter than 180 days, it is suggested to reduce the amount of material rather than to slight systematic review.

HOME STUDY COURSE

While the memory materials in this book have been selected with the Lutheran schools primarily in mind, the arrangement of the book makes it suitable also for home study. Tens of thousands of Lutheran children have no opportunity to attend Lutheran schools, yet the duty of their parents to have them thoroughly grounded in the Word of God is the same as of children who have better opportunities. To such parents it is recommended to set aside fifteen to thirty minutes each day for study with their children, following the outline of the memory course during the school year. The arrangement of the course is simple, and the study of one lesson on every school day will enable the child to complete a year's work during a period of approximately nine months. A copy of the 1943 synodical Catechism will be necessary in the upper grades, for beginning with the fifth grade, Catechism selection and Scripture passages are merely indicated and have to be studied from the source. To be successful, this home work must be done conscientiously and consistently every day. The review lessons are as important as the first learning of the selections. Parents will discuss the selections with their children, explain whenever necessary, and hear the children recite. Great blessings will come to the Church if all parents whose children's opportunities for Christian education are limited will do this. But the greatest blessings will come to the parents and children themselves.

SOURCE BOOKS USED

The materials contained in this book have been selected chiefly from the following sources, which are listed with the abbreviations used to designate them:

Luther's Small Catechism
(Concordia, 1943) _____ Catechism
The Lutheran Hymnal (Concordia, 1941) ___ L. H.
The Bible (King James Version)
Reference to book, chapter, and verse

Minor sources used are listed below:

Educational Guide and Course of Study
(Texas District) _____ Texas Guide
Arcadia Camp Songs (Walther League) ___ A. C. S.
Kirchengesangbuch (Concordia) _____ Kg.
Little Folded Hands (Concordia) _____ L. F. H.
Ev. Luth. Hymn-book (Concordia) _____ H. B.
Music Reader for Lutheran Schools
(Concordia) _____ M. R.
Select Songs for School and Home
(Concordia) _____ S. S.

SUGGESTIONS FROM FIELD

A prospectus of this Memory Course was submitted to all teachers in the Lutheran schools of the Missouri Synod in February, 1943, and their comment, criticism, and suggestions were solicited. Replies were received from individuals, teaching staffs, and conferences, and their encouragement and assistance are herewith gratefully acknowledged.

AUTHORSHIP

THE MEMORY BOOK FOR LUTHERAN SCHOOLS was prepared under the auspices of Synod's Board of Parish Education by a committee of teachers. Members of the committee were H. C. Gruber, E. G. Luepke, Wm. A. Kramer, E. F. Sagehorn, and George C. Stohlmann, chairman. The work was undertaken chiefly to improve the techniques by which the memorizing of religious material might be made meaningful, permanent, pleasant, and generally effective. It is the hope and prayer of the Board of Parish Education and the authors that this purpose may have been attained to a substantial degree. May God's blessing rest on the work of the committee and of others who have contributed in any manner to the effort.

WM. A. KRAMER

HOW
TO MEMORIZE

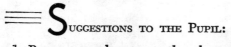SUGGESTIONS TO THE PUPIL:

1. Be sure you know exactly what and how much you are to memorize before you begin.

2. Make every effort to understand the material that is to be memorized.

   a. Read the entire lesson several times and see its meaning as a whole. Reading aloud will help.

   b. State the meaning in your own words. If necessary, outline the lesson.

   c. Try to see the memory gem in your book with your eyes closed.

   d. Write the lesson if you have difficulty in learning it from the printed page.

3. Think of the benefit of the material you are learning.

4. Memorize in a quiet place, where you can concentrate on the lesson.

5. Memorize short selections as wholes rather than as parts.

6. Memorize long selections by parts which have a single general thought; then memorize the connections between the parts. But read the entire selection carefully and thoughtfully several times before studying the parts.

7. Memorize exactly (carelessly memorized material is quickly forgotten; exactness in all things aids character growth).

8. Begin early and memorize in short periods, avoiding a last-minute cramming effort.

9. Review frequently the material you have memorized, even after you know it perfectly ("overlearning" aids the retention of memorized materials).

10. Let someone test you before you recite in school, or test yourself by writing the lesson from memory.

Grade 1

Unit I — God

LESSONS

1. God made all things.

   245. In the beginning God created the heaven and the earth. *Gen. 1:1.*

2. God knows all things.

   296. Lord, Thou knowest all things. *John 21:17.*

3. *Review Lesson 1, 2.*

4. We should worship God.

   54. Thou shalt worship the Lord, thy God,
   and Him only shalt thou serve. *Matt. 4:10.*

5. *Review Lesson 1—4.*

Unit II — Prayer

6. Christians must pray.

   556. Pray without ceasing. *1 Thess. 5:17.*

7, 8. Morning Prayer.

The morning bright with rosy light
Hath waked me up from sleep;
Father, Thy own great love alone
Thy little one doth keep. S. S., *247:1.*

9, 10. All through the day, I humbly pray,
Be Thou my Guard and Guide;
My sins forgive and let me live,
Blest Jesus, near Thy side.

S. S., *247:2.*

11. *Review Lessons 7—10.*

12. *Review Lessons 6—10.*

13. *Review Lessons 1—10.*

14, 15. Evening Prayer.

Now I lay me down to sleep,
I pray Thee, Lord, my soul to keep;
If I should die before I wake,
I pray Thee, Lord, my soul to take;
And this I ask for Jesus' sake. Amen.

M. R., *11.*

16, 17. Evening Prayer.

Jesus, tender Shepherd, hear me:
Bless Thy little lamb tonight;
Through the darkness be Thou near me;
Keep me safe till morning light.

S. S., *262:1.*

18, 19. All this day Thy hand has led me,
  And I thank Thee for Thy care;
  Thou hast clothed me, warmed and
   fed me;
  Listen to my evening prayer.
        S. S., 262:2.

20, 21. May my sins be all forgiven;
  Bless the friends I love so well;
  Take us all at last to heaven,
  Happy there with Thee to dwell.
        S. S., 262:3.

 22. *Review Lessons 16–21.*

 23. *Review Lessons 14–21.*

 24. Prayer before Meals.
  Heavenly Father, bless this food
  To Thy glory and our good. Amen.

 25. Come, Lord Jesus, be our Guest,
  And let Thy gifts to us be blest. Amen.

 26. *Review Lessons 24, 25.*

27, 28. Prayer after Meals.
  Oh, give thanks unto the Lord,
   for He is good;
  Because His mercy endureth forever.
  Amen. *Ps. 118:1.*

 29. *Review Lessons 24–28.*

 30. *Review Lessons 1–10.*

 31. *Review Lessons 14–28.*

Unit III — The Ten Commandments

32. The First Commandment.
    Thou shalt have no other gods before Me.

33. The Second Commandment.
    Thou shalt not take the name
        of the Lord, thy God, in vain.

34. The Third Commandment.
    Remember the Sabbath day,
        to keep it holy.

35, 36. *Review Lessons 32–34. (Commandments 1–3.)*

37, 38. The Fourth Commandment.
    Thou shalt honor thy father and thy
        mother,
    that it may be well with thee,
    and thou mayest live long on the earth.

39. The Fifth Commandment.
    Thou shalt not kill.

40. The Sixth Commandment.
    Thou shalt not commit adultery.

41. The Seventh Commandment.
    Thou shalt not steal.

42. *Review Lessons 37–41. (Commandments 4–7.)*

43. *Review Lessons 32–41. (Commandments 1–7.)*

44. The Eighth Commandment.
Thou shalt not bear false witness against
thy neighbor.

45. The Ninth Commandment.
Thou shalt not covet thy neighbor's
house.

46–48. The Tenth Commandment.
Thou shalt not covet thy neighbor's wife,
nor his manservant,
nor his maidservant,
nor his cattle,
nor anything that is thy neighbor's.

49. *Review Lessons 44–48. (Commandments 8–10.)*

50. *Review Lessons 32–34. (Commandments 1–3.)*

51. *Review Lessons 37–41. (Commandments 4–7.)*

52. *Review Lessons 44–48. (Commandments 8–10.)*

53. *Review Lessons 32–48. (Commandments 1–10.)*

Unit IV — Salvation and Faith

54. Faith saves us.
240. The just shall live by his faith.
Hab. 2:4.

55. 633. He that believeth and is baptized
shall be saved. *Mark 16:16.*

56. 654. Believe on the Lord Jesus Christ,
and thou shalt be saved.
Acts 16:31.

57, 58. *Review Lessons 54–56.*

59. Christ forgives sins.

504. Son, be of good cheer; thy sins be
forgiven thee. *Matt. 9:2.*

60. *Review of Lessons 54–59.*

Unit V — Christmas

61. Christ was born for us.

338. Unto us a Child is born,
unto us a Son is given. *Is. 9:6.*

62, 63. Christmas Prayer.
Ah, dearest Jesus, holy Child,
Make Thee a bed, soft, undefiled,
Within my heart, that it may be
A quiet chamber kept for Thee.
L. H., 85:13.

64. *Review of Lessons 61–63.*

65, 66. Christmas Song.
Let us all with gladsome voice
Praise the God of heaven,
Who, to bid our hearts rejoice,
His own Son hath given. *L. H., 97:1.*

67, 68. To this vale of tears He comes,
　　　Here to serve in sadness,
　　That with Him in heaven's fair homes
　　　We may reign in gladness.

L. H., 97:2.

69. *Review Lessons 65–68.*

70, 71. We are rich, for He was poor;
　　　Is not this a wonder?
　　Therefore praise God evermore
　　　Here on earth and yonder.

L. H., 97:3.

72, 73. O Lord Christ, our Savior dear,
　　　Be Thou ever near us.
　　Grant us now a glad new year.
　　　Amen, Jesus, hear us! *L. H., 97:4.*

74. *Review Lessons 70–73.*

75. *Review Lessons 65–73.*

76. *Review Lessons 61–73.*

Unit VI — Love

77. God loves us.
　　45. God is love. *1 John 4:8.*
　　Jesus loves me, Jesus loves me;
　　　He is always, always near.
　　If I do but trust and love Him,
　　　There is nothing I need fear.

S. S., 260:1.

78. Jesus loves me, and He watches
    Over me with loving eye,
And He sends His holy angels
    Safe to keep me till I die.

                     S. S., 260:4.

79. *Review Lessons 77, 78.*

80, 81. Christians love others.
    Thou shalt love thy neighbor as thyself.
      Matt. 22:39.

    189. By love serve one another. *Gal. 5:13.*
    Christians love their enemies.
    117. Love your enemies.   *Matt. 5:44.*

82. *Review Lessons 77, 78.*

83. *Review Lessons 80, 81.*

84. *Review Lessons 77–81.*

Unit VII — The Creed

85, 86. The First Article.
    I believe in God the Father Almighty,
    Maker of heaven and earth.

87–92. The Second Article.
    And in Jesus Christ, His only Son,
        our Lord,
    who was conceived by the Holy Ghost,
    born of the Virgin Mary,
    suffered under Pontius Pilate,

was crucified, dead, and buried;
He descended into hell;
the third day He rose again from
    the dead;
He ascended into heaven,
and sitteth on the right hand of God
    the Father Almighty;
from thence He shall come to judge
    the quick and the dead.

93–95. The Third Article.
I believe in the Holy Ghost;
the Holy Christian Church,
    the communion of saints;
the forgiveness of sins;
the resurrection of the body;
and the life everlasting. Amen.

96–98. *Review Lessons 85–95. (Articles 1–3.)*

Unit VIII — Prayer

99, 100. Beginning of School Day.
Oh, help me, Lord, this day to be
Thy own dear child, to follow Thee;
And lead me, Savior, by Thy hand
Until I reach the heavenly land. Amen.
                                    L. F. H., 4.

101, 102. Close of School Day.
        Lord Jesus, who dost love me,
        Oh, spread Thy wings above me,
        And shield me from alarm!
        Though evil would assail me,
        Thy mercy will not fail me:
        I rest in Thy protecting arm.
                                    L. H., 554:5.
    103. *Review Lessons 99–102.*

104, 105. Close of School Day.
        Abide, O dearest Jesus,
            Among us with Thy grace
        That Satan may not harm us
            Nor we to sin give place. *L. H.*, 53:1.

    106. *Review Lessons 99–105.*

    107. When Entering Church.
        Create in me a clean heart, O God,
        And renew a right spirit within me.
            Ps. 51:10.

    108. When Leaving Church.
        112. Blessed are they that hear the Word
            of God and keep it.   *Luke 11:28.*

    109. *Review Lessons 107, 108.*

110, 111. General Prayer.
        Lord, teach a little child to pray,
            And, oh, accept my prayer;
        Thou hearest all the words I say,
            For Thou art everywhere. *S. S.*, 257:1.

112, 113. A little sparrow cannot fall
       Unnoticed, Lord, by Thee;
   And though I am so young and small,
       Thou carest still for me.   S. S., 257:2.

114, 115. Teach me to do whate'er is right,
       And when I sin, forgive;
   And make it still my chief delight
       To love Thee while I live.
                        S. S., 275:3.

   116. *Review Lessons 110–115.*

   117. *Review Lessons 99–115.*

118–122. The Lord's Prayer.
   Our Father who art in heaven.
   Hallowed be Thy name.
   Thy kingdom come.
   Thy will be done on earth
     as it is in heaven.
   Give us this day our daily bread.
   And forgive us our trespasses,
   as we forgive those who trespass
     against us.
   And lead us not into temptation.
   But deliver us from evil.
   For Thine is the kingdom and the power
     and the glory forever and ever. Amen.

Unit IX — Obedience

123. We must obey God.

> 66. I am the almighty God;
> walk before Me, and be thou
> perfect. *Gen. 17:1.*

124. We must obey our parents.

> 124. Children, obey your parents in all
> things;
> for this is well pleasing
> unto the Lord. *Col. 3:20.*

125. *Review Lessons 123, 124.*

126. *Review Lessons 1–4.*

Unit X — Sin and Punishment

127. The sinner must die.

> 196. The wages of sin is death. *Rom. 6:23.*

128. God punishes lies.

> 174. He that speaketh lies shall not
> escape. *Prov. 19:5.*

129. *Review Lessons 127, 128.*

Unit XI — The Passion

130. Jesus saved us from sin.

> 314. The blood of Jesus Christ, His Son,
> cleanseth us from all sin.
> *1 John 1:7.*

131. [368.] The Son of Man is come to save that
      which was lost.   *Matt. 18:11.*

132. *Review Lessons 130, 131.*

133, 134. Passion Hymn.

      Let me learn of Jesus;
        He is kind to me;
      Once He died to save me,
        Nailed upon the tree.   S. S., 258:1.

135, 136. If I go to Jesus,
        He will hear me pray,
      Make me pure and holy,
        Take my sins away.   S. S., 258:2.

137, 138. Oh, how good is Jesus!
        May He hold my hand,
      And at last receive me
        To a better land.   S. S., 258:5.

139. *Review Lessons 133–138.*

140. *Review Lessons 130–138.*

Unit XII — Baptism

141–143. Which is that word of God?

      Christ, our Lord, says in the last chapter
        of Matthew:
      Go ye and teach all nations,
      baptizing them in the name of the Father
        and of the Son and of the Holy Ghost.

144–146. Which are such words and promises of God?
　　　　Christ, our Lord, says in the last chapter
　　　　　　of Mark:
　　　　He that believeth and is baptized
　　　　　　shall be saved;
　　　　but he that believeth not
　　　　　　shall be damned.

147, 148. *Review Lessons 141–146.*

Unit XIII — Review

　　149. *Review Lessons 1–4.*

　　150. *Review Lessons 6–10.*

　　151. *Review Lessons 14–17.*

　　152. *Review Lessons 18–21.*

　　153. *Review Lessons 14–21.*

　　154. *Review Lessons 24–28.*

　　155. *Review Lessons 32–34.*

　　156. *Review Lessons 37–41.*

　　157. *Review Lessons 44–48.*

　　158. *Review Lessons 32–48.*

　　159. *Review Lessons 54–56.*

　　160. *Review Lessons 54–59.*

　　161. *Review Lessons 61–63.*

　　162. *Review Lessons 65–68.*

163. *Review Lessons 70–73.*

164. *Review Lessons 61–73.*

165. *Review Lessons 77, 78.*

166. *Review Lessons 77–81.*

167–169. *Review Lessons 85–95.*

170. *Review Lessons 99–102.*

171. *Review Lessons 104, 105, 107, 108.*

172. *Review Lessons 110–113.*

173. *Review Lessons 110–115.*

174. *Review Lessons 118–122.*

175. *Review Lessons 123, 124, 127, 128*

176. *Review Lessons 130, 131.*

177. *Review Lessons 133–138.*

178. *Review Lessons 141–143.*

179. *Review Lessons 144–146.*

180. *Review Lessons 141–146.*

Grade 2

Unit 1 — God

LESSONS

1. *Review Grade I, Lessons 1–4.*

2. God is holy.
   39. Holy, holy, holy, is the Lord of hosts. *Is. 6:3.*

3. God has no body.
   God is a spirit. *John 4:24.*

4. God can do anything.
   33. With God nothing shall be impossible. *Luke 1:37.*

5. 297. All power is given unto Me in heaven and in earth. *Matt. 28:18.*

6. God is always with us.
   295. Lo, I am with you alway, even unto the end of the world. *Matt. 28:20.*

7. *Review Lessons 2–6.*

Unit II — Prayer

8. *Review Grade I, Lessons 6–10.*

9. *Review Grade I, Lessons 14–17.*

10. *Review Grade I, Lessons 14–21.*

29

11. *Review Grade I, Lessons 24–28.*

12. *Review Grade I, Lessons 99–102.*

13. *Review Grade I, Lessons 104–108.*

14. *Review Grade I, Lessons 110–115.*

15. *Review Grade I, Lessons 118–122.*

16. God will hear us in trouble.
    93. Call upon Me in the day of trouble.
        I will deliver thee,
        and thou shalt glorify Me. *Ps. 50:15.*

17. 271. Cast all your care upon Him;
        for He careth for you. *1 Pet. 5:7.*

18. 696. Him that cometh to Me I will in no
        wise cast out. *John 6:37.*

19. *Review Lessons 16–18.*

20. We must speak of God's goodness.
    95. Bless the Lord, O my soul,
        and all that is within me, bless His
        holy name. *Ps. 103:1.*

21. We must thank God for His goodness.
    96. O give thanks unto the Lord,
            for He is good;
        because His mercy endureth forever.
            Ps. 118:1.

22. *Review Lessons 20, 21.*

23. *Review Lessons 16–21.*

24, 25. Morning Prayer.
Lord God, I thank Thee for the light,
For Thy protection through the night;
Thou gavest rest and quiet sleep
While holy angels watch did keep.
M. R., 76:1.

26, 27. Guard and protect me through the day,
Guide and direct my work and play;
Throughout this day my thought shall be:
Thou, heavenly Father, seest me.
M. R., 76:2.

28. *Review Lessons 24–27.*

29. Evening Prayer.
Now the light has gone away;
Father, listen while I pray,
Asking Thee to watch and keep
And to send me quiet sleep.
L. H., 653:1.

30. Jesus, Savior, wash away
All that has been wrong today;
Help me every day to be
Good and gentle, more like Thee.
L. H., 653:2.

31. Let my near and dear ones be
    Always near and dear to Thee;
    Oh, bring me and all I love
    To Thy happy home above.

32, 33. *Review Lessons 29–31.*   *L. H., 653:3.*

34. *Review Lessons 24–31.*

Unit III — God's Word

35. The Bible is never wrong.

    7. The Scripture cannot be broken.
       John 10:35.

36. God's Word shows us what to believe and how
    to live.

    9. Thy Word is a lamp unto my feet and
       a light unto my path. *Ps. 119:105.*

37. *Review Lessons 35, 36.*

Unit IV — Review of the Ten Commandments and Creed (text only)

38, 39. *Review Grade I, Lessons 32–48.*

40, 41. *Review Grade I, Lessons 85–95.*

Unit V — The First Article

42–49. The First Article.

    I believe in God the Father Almighty,
    Maker of heaven and earth.

    What does this mean? I believe that God

has made me and all creatures; that He has given me my body and soul, eyes, ears, and all my members, my reason and all my senses, and still preserves them;

also clothing and shoes, meat and drink, house and home, wife and children, fields, cattle, and all my goods; that He richly and daily provides me with all that I need to support this body and life;

that He defends me against all danger, and guards and protects me from all evil;

and all this purely out of fatherly, divine goodness and mercy, without any merit or worthiness in me;

for all which it is my duty to thank and praise, to serve and obey Him.

This is most certainly true.

Unit VI — Salvation and Faith

50. *Review Grade I, Lessons 54–59.*
51. God wants to save us.
    571. Fear not, little flock;
    for it is your Father's good pleasure to give you the Kingdom.
    Luke 12:32.

52. Jesus forgives sins.

> [300.] The Son of Man hath power on earth to forgive sins.   *Matt. 9:6.*

53. [352.] Behold the Lamb of God, which taketh away the sin of the world. *John 1:29.*

54. *Review Lessons 51–53.*

55. Those who believe in Jesus are saved.

> [241.] Thy faith hath saved thee; go in peace.   *Luke 7:50.*

56. We must believe until death.

> [524.] He that shall endure unto the end, the same shall be saved. *Matt. 24:13.*

57. *Review Lessons 55, 56.*

58. *Review Lessons 51–56.*

Unit VII — The Second Article

59–66. The Second Article.

> And in Jesus Christ, His only Son, our Lord, who was conceived by the Holy Ghost, born of the Virgin Mary, suffered under Pontius Pilate, was crucified, dead, and buried;

He descended into hell; the third day He rose again from the dead; He ascended into heaven, and sitteth on the right hand of God the Father Almighty; from thence He shall come to judge the quick and the dead.

What does this mean? I believe that Jesus Christ, true God, begotten of the Father from eternity, and also true man, born of the Virgin Mary, is my Lord,

who has redeemed me, a lost and condemned creature, purchased and won me from all sins, from death, and from the power of the devil; not with gold or silver, but with His holy, precious blood and with His innocent suffering and death,

that I may be His own, and live under Him in His kingdom, and serve Him in everlasting righteousness, innocence, and blessedness,

even as He is risen from the dead, lives and reigns to all eternity.

This is most certainly true.

67. *Review Lessons 42–49.*

Unit VIII — Christmas

68. *Review Grade I, Lessons 61–63.*

69. *Review Grade I, Lessons 65–73.*

70. A Christmas Hymn.

As each happy Christmas
    Dawns on earth again,
Comes the holy Christ Child
    To the hearts of men,   S. S., 242:1.

71. Enters with His blessing
    Into every home,
Guides and guards our footsteps
    As we go and come.   S. S., 242:2.

72. All unknown, beside me
    He will ever stand,
And will safely lead me
    With His own right hand.   S. S., 242:3.

73. *Review Lessons 70–72.*

Unit IX — Love

74. *Review Grade I, Lessons 77–81.*

75. God loves us.

18. God so loved the world that He gave
        His only-begotten Son,
    that whosoever believeth in Him
        should not perish,
    but have everlasting life.   *John 3:16.*

76. We should love God.

Thou shalt love the Lord, thy God,
with all thy heart and with all thy soul
and with all thy mind. *Matt. 22:37.*

77. *Review Lessons 75, 76.*

Unit X — Trust

78. God wants us to trust in Him.

72. Trust in the Lord with all thine
heart. *Prov. 3:5.*

79, 80. A Song of Trust.

I am Jesus' little lamb,
Ever glad at heart I am;
For my Shepherd gently guides me,
Knows my need and well provides me,
Loves me every day the same,
Even calls me by my name.

L. H., 648:1.

81, 82. Day by day, at home, away,
Jesus is my Staff and Stay.
When I hunger, Jesus feeds me,
Into pleasant pastures leads me;
When I thirst, He bids me go
Where the quiet waters flow.

L. H., 648:2.

83, 84. Who so happy as I am,
        Even now the Shepherd's lamb?
        And when my short life is ended,
        By His angel host attended,
        He shall fold me to His breast,
        There within His arms to rest.

85, 86. *Review Lessons 78–84.*   *L. H., 648:3.*

Unit XI — The Sacrament of the Altar

87–94. Where is this written?

The holy Evangelists Matthew, Mark, Luke, and St. Paul [the Apostle] write thus:

Our Lord Jesus Christ, the same night in which He was betrayed, took bread; and when He had given thanks, He brake it and gave it to His disciples, saying, Take, eat; this is My body, which is given for you. This do in remembrance of Me.

After the same manner also He took the cup when He had supped, and when He had given thanks, He gave it to them, saying, Drink ye all of it; this cup is the new testament in My blood, which is shed for you for the remission of sins. This do, as oft as ye drink it, in remembrance of Me.

Unit XII — Obedience

95. *Review Grade I, Lessons 123, 124.*

96. We must obey God above all.

> 127. We ought to obey God rather than men. *Acts 5:29.*

97. Love makes us obey God.

> 13. If a man love Me, he will keep My words. *John 14:23.*

98. *Review Lessons 96, 97.*

Unit XIII — Prayer

99. Prayer before Meals.

> Thou openest Thine hand, O Lord,
>> The earth is filled with good;
> Teach us with thankful hearts to take
>> From Thee our daily food. Amen.

100. Prayer after Meals.   *A. C. S., 55.*

> We thank Thee, Lord, for all the food,
> For life and health and every good.
>> Amen.

101. *Review Lessons 99, 100.*

102. At Beginning of School Day.

> Father, bless our school today;
> Be in all we do or say;
> Be in every song we sing,
> Every prayer to Thee we bring.
>> *S. S., 77:1.*

103. Jesus, well-beloved Son,
    May Thy will by us be done;
    Come and meet with us today;
    Teach us, Lord, Thyself, to pray.
                      S. S., 77:2.

104. *Review Lessons 102, 103.*

105. At Close of School Day.
    Abide, O faithful Savior,
      Among us with Thy love;
    Grant steadfastness and help us
      To reach our home above.
                      L. H., 53:6.

106. *Review Lessons 102–105.*

107. Prayer upon Entering Church.
    Lord, open Thou my heart to hear,
    And through Thy Word to me draw near;
    Let me Thy Word e'er pure retain,
    Let me Thy child and heir remain.
                      L. H., 5:1.

108. Prayer before Leaving Church.
    Abide, O dear Redeemer,
      Among us with Thy Word,
    And thus now and hereafter
      True peace and joy afford.
                      L. H., 53:2.

109. *Review Lessons 107, 108.*

110. Song of Praise.
   Praise God, from whom all blessings flow;
   Praise Him, all creatures here below;
   Praise Him above, ye heavenly host:
   Praise Father, Son, and Holy Ghost.

   L. H., 644.

111. Prayer in Sickness.
   Tender Jesus, meek and mild,
   Look on me, a little child,
   Help me, if it is Thy will
   To recover from all ill.

   L. F. H., 64.

112. *Review Lessons 110, 111.*

113, 114. Prayer for a Peaceful Death.
   I fall asleep in Jesus' wounds,
   There pardon for my sins abounds;
   Yea, Jesus' blood and righteousness
   My jewels are, my glorious dress.
   In these before my God I'll stand
   When I shall reach the heavenly land.

   L. H., 585:1.

115. *Review Lessons 110–114.*

116. *Review Lessons 99, 100.*

117. *Review Lessons 102–105.*

118. *Review Lessons 107, 108.*

119. *Review Lessons 110, 111.*

120. *Review Lessons 113, 114.*

121. *Review Lessons 99–114.*

Unit XIV — Sin and Punishment

122. *Review Grade I, Lessons 127, 128.*

123. God wants us to be without sin.

> 14. Ye shall be holy;
>   for I, the Lord, your God, am holy.
>   *Lev. 19:2.*

124. 193. Be ye therefore perfect,
>   even as your Father which is in
>   heaven is perfect. *Matt. 5:48.*

125. It is sin to borrow and not pay back.

> 164. The wicked borroweth and payeth
>   not again. *Ps. 37:21.*

126. Speaking evil of others is sin.

> 177. Speak not evil one of another,
>   brethren. *James 4:11.*

127. *Review Lessons 123–126.*

128. God punishes those who kill.

> 129. All they that take the sword shall
>   perish with the sword.
>   *Matt. 26:52.*

129. God punishes laziness.

> 163. If any would not work, neither
>   should he eat. *2 Thess. 3:10.*

130. God warns us against the devil.

> 361. Resist the devil, and he will flee from you.   *James 4:7.*

131. *Review Lessons 128–130.*

132. *Review Lessons 123–130.*

Unit XV — The Passion

133, 134. *Review Grade I, Lessons 130–138.*

135. A Passion Hymn.

> There is a green hill far away,
>   Without a city wall,
> Where the dear Lord was crucified,
>   Who died to save us all.
>
> S. S., 38:1.

136. He died that we might be forgiven,
>   He died to make us good,
> That we might go at last to heaven,
>   Saved by His precious blood.
>
> S. S., 38:3.

137. Oh, dearly, dearly He has loved!
>   And we must love Him, too,
> And trust in His redeeming blood
>   And try His works to do.
>
> S. S., 38:5.

138. *Review Lessons 135–137.*

Unit XVI — Review

139. *Review Lessons 2–4.*
140. *Review Lessons 2–6.*
141. *Review Lessons 16–18.*
142. *Review Lessons 20, 21.*
143. *Review Lessons 24–27.*
144. *Review Lessons 29–31.*
145. *Review Lessons 35, 36, 96, 97.*
146–148. *Review Lessons 42–49.*
149. *Review Lessons 51–53.*
150. *Review Lessons 51–56.*
151–153. *Review Lessons 59–66.*
154. *Review Lessons 70–72.*
155. *Review Lessons 75, 76.*
156. *Review Lessons 79, 80.*
157. *Review Lessons 81, 82.*
158. *Review Lessons 83, 84.*
159. *Review Lessons 79–84.*
160–162. *Review Lessons 87–94.*
163. *Review Lessons 99, 100.*
164. *Review Lessons 102, 103.*
165. *Review Lessons 102–105.*
166. *Review Lessons 107, 108.*
167. *Review Lessons 110, 111.*
168. *Review Lessons 113, 114.*

Unit XVII — The End of the World

169. The end of the world is near.

> 403. The end of all things is at hand.
>   *1 Peter 4:7.*

Unit XVIII — Pentecost: Mission Work

170. *Review Grade I, Lessons 141–143.*

171. *Review Grade I, Lessons 144–146.*

172. Christians must show others the way to heaven.

> 48. Go ye, therefore, and teach
>   all nations,
>   baptizing them in the name of the
>   Father and of the Son and of the
>   Holy Ghost.   *Matt. 28:19.*

173. *Review Lessons 169, 172.*

Unit XIX — Review

174. *Review Lessons 99–105.*

175. *Review Lessons 107–114.*

176. *Review Lessons 123–126.*

177. *Review Lessons 123–130.*

178. *Review Lessons 135, 136.*

179. *Review Lessons 135–137.*

180. *Review Lessons 169, 172.*

Grade 3

Unit I — God

LESSONS

1. *Review Grade I, Lessons 1–4.*

2. *Review Grade II, Lessons 2–6.*

3. God made us.

   243. Have we not all one Father?
        Hath not one God created us?
        Mal. 2:10.

   God made all things.

   22. Every house is builded by some man;
       but He that built all things is God.
       Heb. 3:4.

4. God keeps us.

   268. O Lord, Thou preservest man and
        beast. *Ps. 36:6.*

   269. He upholds all things by the word
        of His power. *Heb. 1:3.*

5. *Review Lessons 3, 4.*

6. Jesus is God.

   289. This is the true God and eternal life.
        1 John 5:20.

324. This is My beloved Son, in whom I am well pleased; hear ye Him. *Matt. 17:5.*

7. Jesus will judge the world.

395. He is ordained of God to be the Judge of quick and dead. *Acts 10:42.*

8. *Review Lessons 6, 7.*

9. *Review Lessons 3–7.*

Unit II — Prayer

10. *Review Grade I, Lessons 6–21.*

11. *Review Grade I, Lessons 24–28; 99–105.*

12. *Review Grade I, Lessons 107–122.*

13. *Review Grade II, Lessons 16–21.*

14. *Review Grade II, Lessons 24–31.*

15. *Review Grade II, Lessons 99–105.*

16. *Review Grade II, Lessons 107–114.*

17, 18. God promises to hear our prayers.

94. Ask, and it shall be given you;
seek, and ye shall find;
knock, and it shall be opened unto you. *Matt. 7:7.*

*238. Commit thy way unto the Lord;
     trust also in Him;
     and He shall bring it to pass.
          Ps. 37:5.

534. O Thou that hearest prayer, unto
     Thee shall all flesh come. *Ps. 65:2.*

19. Morning Prayer.

All praise to Thee, who safe hast kept
And hast refreshed me while I slept.
Grant, Lord, when I from death shall
     wake,
I may of endless light partake.
                              L. H., 536:3.

20. Prayer before Meals.

The eyes of all wait upon Thee, O Lord,
and Thou givest them their meat
     in due season.
Thou openest Thine hand
and satisfiest the desire of every living
     thing. *Ps. 145:15, 16.*

21. Prayer after Meals.

We thank Thee, Lord God, heavenly
     Father,
through Jesus Christ, our Lord,
for all Thy benefits,
who livest and reignest forever and ever.
     Amen.

22. *Review Lessons 17–21.*

23. At Close of School Day.

Bless our going out, we pray,
   Bless our entrance in like measure;
Bless our bread, O Lord, each day,
   Bless our toil, our rest, our pleasure;
Bless us when we reach death's portal,
Bless us then with life immortal.

L. H., 45:3.

24. Upon Entering Church.

Lord Jesus, bless the pastor's word,
   And bless my hearing, too,
That after all is said and heard,
   I may believe and do. Amen.

Texas Guide, p. 28.

25. Upon Leaving Church.

Abide with heavenly brightness
   Among us, precious Light;
Thy truth direct and keep us
   From error's gloomy night.

L. H., 53:3.

26. Abide with richest blessings
   Among us, bounteous Lord;
Let us in grace and wisdom
   Grow daily through Thy Word.

L. H., 53:4.

27. Abide with Thy protection
      Among us, Lord, our Strength,
   Lest world and Satan fell us
      And overcome at length.

28. *Review Lessons 23–27.*   *L. H., 53:5.*

29. *Review Lessons 17–21.*

30. *Review Lessons 23–27.*

Unit III — God's Word

31. *Review Grade II, Lessons 35, 36.*

32. God told men what to write in the Bible.

   2. All Scripture is given by inspiration
      of God.   *2 Tim. 3:16.*

  The Bible is never wrong.

   562. Sanctify them through Thy truth;
      Thy Word is truth.   *John 17:17.*

33. Christians love God's Word.

   103. He that is of God heareth God's
      words;

     ye therefore hear them not because
     ye are not of God.   *John 8:47.*

34. *Review Lessons 32, 33.*

35. Christians use God's Word.

   110. Let the Word of Christ dwell in you
      richly.   *Col. 3:16.*

*475. If ye continue in My Word, then
are ye My disciples indeed;
and ye shall know the truth,
and the truth shall make you free.
John 8:31, 32.

36. The Bible shows us what sin is.
211. By the Law is the knowledge of sin.
Rom. 3:20.

37. A Hymn about God's Word.
How precious is the Book Divine,
By inspiration given!
Bright as a lamp its doctrines shine
To guide our souls to heaven.
L. H., 285:1.

38. *Review Lessons 35–37.*

39. *Review Lessons 32–37.*

Unit IV — Catechism Review

40, 41. *Review Grade I, Lessons 141–146.*

42–47. *Review Grade II, Lessons 42–49; 59–66
(Articles I and II).*

48–51. *Review Grade II, Lessons 87–94
(Sixth Chief Part: Where is this written?).*

Unit V — Salvation and Faith

52. *Review Grade I, Lessons 54–59.*

53. *Review Grade II, Lessons 51–56.*

54. God wants to save all people.
> 454. God will have all men to be saved and to come unto the knowledge of the truth. *1 Tim. 2:4.*

55. Only God can make me a believer.
> 432. Turn Thou me, and I shall be turned; for Thou art the Lord, my God. *Jer. 31:18.*
>
> Only the believer can please God.
> 443. Without faith it is impossible to please Him. *Heb. 11:6.*

56. By Baptism our sins are forgiven.
> 617. Arise and be baptized and wash away thy sins. *Acts 22:16.*

57. We must forgive our neighbor.
> 139. If ye forgive not men their trespasses, neither will your Father forgive your trespasses. *Matt. 6:15.*

58. *Review Lessons 54–57.*

59. A Hymn of Faith.
> Rock of Ages, cleft for me,
> Let me hide myself in Thee;
> Let the water and the blood
> From Thy riven side which flowed
> Be of sin the double cure,
> Cleanse me from its guilt and power.
>
> *L. H., 376:1.*

60. Not the labors of my hands
    Can fulfill Thy Law's demands;
    Could my zeal no respite know,
    Could my tears forever flow,
    All for sin could not atone;
    Thou must save, and Thou alone.

    L. H., 376:2.

61. *Review Lessons 59, 60.*

62. Nothing in my hand I bring,
    Simply to Thy cross I cling;
    Naked, come to Thee for dress;
    Helpless, look to Thee for grace;
    Foul, I to the fountain fly —
    Wash me, Savior, or I die.

    L. H., 376:3.

63. While I draw this fleeting breath,
    When mine eyelids close in death,
    When I soar to worlds unknown,
    See Thee on Thy judgment throne,
    Rock of Ages, cleft for me,
    Let me hide myself in Thee.

    L. H., 376:4.

64. *Review Lessons 62, 63.*

65. *Review Lessons 59–63.*

66. *Review Lessons 54–63.*

Unit VI — Christmas

67. *Review Grade I, Lessons 61–73.*

68. *Review Grade II, Lessons 70–72.*

69. A Christmas Hymn.
"From heaven above to earth I come
To bear good news to every home;
Glad tidings of great joy I bring,
Whereof I now will say and sing.
L. H., 85:1.

70. "To you this night is born a child
Of Mary, chosen virgin mild;
This little child, of lowly birth,
Shall be the joy of all the earth.
L. H., 85:2.

71. "This is the Christ, our God and Lord,
Who in all need shall aid afford;
He will Himself your Savior be
From all your sins to set you free."
L. H., 85:3.

72. Welcome to earth, Thou noble Guest,
Through whom the sinful world is blest!
Thou com'st to share our misery;
What thanks shall I return to Thee?
L. H., 85:8.

73. *Review Lessons 69–72.*

Unit VII — Love

74. *Review Grade I, Lessons 77–81.*

75. *Review Grade II, Lessons 75, 76.*

76. God loves us.
    42. The Lord is good to all,
    and His tender mercies are over all
    His works.   *Ps. 145:9.*

77. 277. Like as a father pitieth his children,
    so the Lord pitieth them that fear
    Him.   *Ps. 103:13.*

78. Christians love others and help them.
    169. Give to him that asketh thee,
    and from him that would borrow of
    thee turn not thou away.
    Matt. 5:42.

79. Love helps us overlook our neighbor's faults.
    183. Charity shall cover the multitude of
    sins.   *1 Pet. 4:8.*

80. *Review Lessons 76–79.*

Unit VIII — Trust

81, 82. *Review Grade II, Lessons 78–84.*

83, 84. God cares for us.
    276. My times are in Thy hand.   *Ps. 31:15.*
    It is best to trust in God.

71. It is better to trust in the Lord than to put confidence in man.

Ps. 118:8.

God sends trouble for our good.

527. We know that all things work together for good to them that love God. *Rom. 8:28.*

Unit IX — The Ten Commandments (First Chief Part)

85. The First Commandment.

Thou shalt have no other gods before Me. *What does this mean?* We should fear, love, and trust in God above all things.

86, 87. The Second Commandment.

Thou shalt not take the name of the Lord, thy God, in vain.

What does this mean? We should fear and love God that we may not curse, swear, use witchcraft, lie, or deceive by His name, but call upon it in every trouble, pray, praise, and give thanks.

88, 89. The Third Commandment.

Remember the Sabbath day, to keep it holy.

(Thou shalt sanctify the holy day.)

What does this mean? We should fear and love God that we may not despise preaching and His Word, but hold it sacred and gladly hear and learn it.

90. *Review Lessons 85–89. (Commandments 1–3.)*

91, 92. The Fourth Commandment.

Thou shalt honor thy father and thy mother, that it may be well with thee, and thou mayest live long on the earth.

What does this mean? We should fear and love God that we may not despise our parents and masters, nor provoke them to anger, but give them honor, serve and obey them, and hold them in love and esteem.

93, 94. The Fifth Commandment.

Thou shalt not kill.

What does this mean? We should fear and love God that we may not hurt nor harm our neighbor in his body, but help and befriend him in every bodily need.

95. *Review Lessons 91–94. (Commandments 4, 5.)*

96, 97. The Sixth Commandment.

Thou shalt not commit adultery.

What does this mean? We should fear and love God that we may lead a chaste and decent life in word and deed, and each love and honor his spouse.

98, 99. The Seventh Commandment.

Thou shalt not steal.

What does this mean? We should fear and love God that we may not take our neighbor's money or goods, nor get them by false ware or dealing, but help him to improve and protect his property and business.

100. *Review Lessons 96–99. (Commandments 6, 7.)*

101, 102. The Eighth Commandment.

Thou shalt not bear false witness against thy neighbor.

What does this mean? We should fear and love God that we may not deceitfully belie, betray, slander, nor defame our neighbor, but defend him, speak well of him, and put the best construction on everything.

103, 104. The Ninth Commandment.

Thou shalt not covet thy neighbor's house.

What does this mean? We should fear and love God that we may not craftily seek to get our neighbor's inheritance or house, nor obtain it by a show of right, but help and be of service to him in keeping it.

105. *Review Lessons 101–104.*
(Commandments 8, 9.)

106, 107. The Tenth Commandment.

Thou shalt not covet thy neighbor's wife, nor his manservant, nor his maidservant, nor his cattle, nor anything that is thy neighbor's.

What does this mean? We should fear and love God that we may not estrange, force, or entice away from our neighbor his wife, servants, or cattle, but urge them to stay and do their duty.

108–112. The Close of the Commandments.

What does God say of all these Commandments? He says thus: I, the Lord, thy God, am a jealous God, visiting the iniquity of the fathers upon the children unto the third and fourth generation of them that hate Me, and showing mercy unto thousands of them that love Me and keep My Commandments.

What does this mean? God threatens to punish all that transgress these Commandments. Therefore we should fear His wrath and not act contrary to them. But He promises grace and every blessing to all that keep these Commandments. Therefore we should also love and trust in Him and willingly do according to His Commandments.

113. *Review Lessons 106–112.*
     (Tenth Commandment, Close.)

114. *Review Lessons 85–89. (Commandments 1–3.)*

115. *Review Lessons 91–94. (Commandments 4, 5.)*

116. *Review Lessons 96–99. (Commandments 6, 7.)*

117. *Review Lessons 101–104.*
     (Commandments 8, 9.)

118. *Review Lessons 106–112.*
     (Tenth Commandment, Close.)

Unit X — The Angels

119. The angels watch over the believers.

255. He shall give His angels charge over thee to keep thee in all thy ways.
     They shall bear thee up in their hands
     lest thou dash thy foot against a stone.   *Ps. 91:11, 12.*

Unit XI — Sin and Punishment

120, 121. *Review Grade I, Lessons 127, 128;*
Grade II, Lessons 123–130.

122. All men are sinners.
204. There is not a just man upon earth
that doeth good and sinneth not.
Eccl. 7:20.

123. Helping a thief makes us thieves.
165. Whoso is partner with a thief hateth
his own soul. *Prov. 29:24.*

124. We must tell the truth; lying is sin.
175. Putting away lying, speak every man
truth with his neighbor;
for we are members one of another.
Eph. 4:25.

125. We must not think evil of our neighbor.
181. Let none of you imagine evil in your
hearts against his neighbor.
Zech. 8:17.

126. God expects us to do good wherever we can.
231. To him that knoweth to do good and
doeth it not,
to him it is sin. *James 4:17.*

127. *Review Lessons 122–126.*

Unit XII — The Passion

128. *Review Grade I, Lessons 130–138.*

129. *Review Grade II, Lessons 135–137.*

130. Christ died for us.

> 328. Christ died for our sins according to the Scriptures.   *1 Cor. 15:3.*
>
> 371. He died for all.   *2 Cor. 5:15.*

131. A Hymn of the Redeemer.

> How sweet the name of Jesus sounds
>   In a believer's ear!
> It soothes his sorrows, heals his wounds,
>   And drives away his fear.
>
> *L. H., 364:1.*

132. It makes the wounded spirit whole
>   And calms the troubled breast;
> 'Tis manna to the hungry soul
>   And to the weary, rest. *L. H., 364:2.*

133. Dear name! The Rock on which I build,
>   My Shield and Hiding Place;
> My never-failing Treasury, filled
>   With boundless stores of grace.
>
> *L. H., 364:3.*

134. *Review Lessons 130–133.*

Unit XIII — Easter

135. An Easter Hymn.

> I know that my Redeemer lives;
> What comfort this sweet sentence gives!
> He lives, He lives, who once was dead;
> He lives, my ever-living Head.
>
> *L. H., 200:1.*

136. He lives to bless me with His love,
> He lives to plead for me above,
> He lives my hungry soul to feed,
> He lives to help in time of need.
>
> *L. H., 200:3.*

137. He lives and grants me daily breath;
> He lives, and I shall conquer death;
> He lives my mansion to prepare;
> He lives to bring me safely there.
>
> *L. H., 200:7.*

138. *Review Lessons 135–137.*

Unit XIV — Obedience

139. *Review Grade I, Lessons 123, 124;*
> *Grade II, Lessons 96, 97.*

140, 141. The obedient Christian hates sin.

> 67. How, then, can I do this great
> wickedness and sin against God?
> *Gen. 39:9.*

68. The fear of the Lord is to hate evil.
   Prov. 8:13.

We must not let evil people mislead us.

158. My son, if sinners entice thee,
   consent thou not.   *Prov. 1:10.*

142. A Hymn of Obedience.
   Jesus, lead Thou on
   Till our rest is won;
   And although the way be cheerless,
   We will follow calm and fearless.
   Guide us by Thy hand
   To our fatherland.   *L. H., 410:1.*

143. If the way be drear,
   If the Foe be near,
   Let not faithless fears o'ertake us;
   Let not faith and hope forsake us;
   For through many a woe
   To our home we go.   *L. H., 410:2.*

*144. When we seek relief
   From a long-felt grief;
   When temptations come alluring;
   Make us patient and enduring;
   Show us that bright shore
   Where we weep no more.   *L. H., 410:3.*

145. Jesus, lead Thou on
Till our rest is won.
Heavenly Leader, still direct us,
Still support, control, protect us,
Till we safely stand
In our fatherland.

                                        L. H., 410:4.

146. *Review Lessons 142–145.*

147. *Review Lessons 140–145.*

Unit XV — Review

148. *Review Lessons 3, 4.*

149. *Review Lessons 6, 7.*

150. *Review Lessons 17–19.*

151. *Review Lessons 20–23.*

152. *Review Lessons 24–27.*

153. *Review Lessons 32, 33.*

154. *Review Lessons 35–37.*

155. *Review Lessons 54–57.*

156. *Review Lessons 59–63.*

157. *Review Lessons 69–72.*

158. *Review Lessons 76–79.*

159. *Review Lessons 83, 84.*

160. *Review Lessons 85–89.*
(Commandments 1–3.)

161. *Review Lessons 91–94.*
(Commandments 4, 5.)

162. *Review Lessons 96–99.*
(Commandments 6, 7.)

163. *Review Lessons 101–104.*
(Commandments 8, 9.)

164. *Review Lessons 106–112.*
(Tenth Commandment, Close.)

165. *Review Lessons 85–99.*
(Commandments 1–7.)

166. *Review Lessons 101–112.*
(Commandment 8 to Close.)

167. *Review Lessons 85–112. (First Chief Part.)*

Unit XVI — Pentecost: Mission Work

168. *Review Grade I, Lessons 141–146;*
Grade II, Lessons 169, 172.

169. A Hymn of Pentecost.
Holy Spirit, hear us
   On this sacred day;
Come to us with blessing,
   Come with us to stay.   *L. H., 229:1.*

170. Come as Thou once camest
     To the faithful few
     Patiently awaiting
     Jesus' promise true.   *L. H.*, 229:2.

171. Up to heaven ascending,
     Our dear Lord has gone;
     Yet His little children
     Leaves He not alone.   *L. H.*, 229:3.

172. To His blessed promise
     Now in faith we cling.
     Comforter, most holy,
     Spread o'er us Thy wing.
                              L. H., 229:4.

173. We must show others the way to heaven.
     115. Go ye into all the world and preach
          the Gospel to every creature.
          Mark 16:15.

174. *Review Lessons 169–173.*

Unit XVII — Review

175. *Review Lessons 119–126.*

176. *Review Lessons 130–133.*

177. *Review Lessons 135–137.*

178. *Review Lessons 140–143.*

179. *Review Lessons 140–145.*

180. *Review Lessons 169–173.*

MEMORY SELECTIONS

Grade 4

Unit I — God

LESSONS

1. *Review Grade I, Lessons 1–4; Grade II, Lessons 2–6.*

2. *Review Grade III, Lessons 3–7.*

3. There is only one God.

   * 27. The Lord is the true God,
   He is the living God and an everlasting King. *Jer. 10:10.*

   46. Hear, O Israel:
   The Lord, our God, is one Lord. *Deut. 6:4.*

   God does not change.

   31. Thou art the same, and Thy years shall have no end. *Ps. 102:27.*

4. God made man.

   261. The Lord God formed man of the dust of the ground
   and breathed into his nostrils the breath of life;
   and man became a living soul. *Gen. 2:7.*

   God made all things.

   247. By Him were all things created that are in heaven and that are in earth, visible and invisible. *Col. 1:16.*

5. *Review Lessons 3, 4.*

6. God's works are wonderful.

   267. I will praise Thee;
   for I am fearfully and wonderfully made;
   marvelous are Thy works;
   and that my soul knoweth right well.
       Ps. 139:14.

   *God keeps us.

   585. He maketh His sun to rise on the evil and
   on the good
   and sendeth rain on the just and on the
   unjust. *Matt. 5:45.*

7. Jesus is God with the Father.

   57. All men should honor the Son even as they
   honor the Father.
   He that honoreth not the Son honoreth not
   the Father, which hath sent Him.
   John 5:23.

   74. This is His name whereby He shall be
   called,
   The Lord our Righteousness. *Jer. 23:6.*

8. *Jesus is Lord over all.

   97. The Son of Man is Lord even of the
   Sabbath day. *Matt. 12:8.*

   Jesus never changes.

   294. Jesus Christ the same yesterday and today
   and forever. *Heb. 13:8.*

9. *Review Lessons 6–8.*

10. *Review Lessons 3–8.*

Unit II — Prayer

11. *Review Grade I, Lessons 6–28.*

12. *Review Grade I, Lessons 99–122.*

13. *Review Grade II, Lessons 16–31.*

14. *Review Grade II, Lessons 99–114.*

15. *Review Grade III, Lessons 17–21.*

16. *Review Grade III, Lessons 23–27.*

17. Prayer must be sincere.

> 530. When ye pray, use not vain repetitions, as the heathen do;
> for they think that they shall be heard for their much speaking.   *Matt. 6:7.*

God answers prayer.

> 532. And it shall come to pass that, before they call, I will answer;
> and while they are yet speaking, I will hear. *Is. 65:24.*

18. God answers prayer.

> 543. This is the confidence that we have in Him, that, if we ask anything according to His will, He heareth us.   *1 John 5:14.*

> 544. Verily, verily, I say unto you,
> Whatsoever ye shall ask the Father in My name, He will give it you.   *John 16:23.*

19. *Review Lessons 17, 18.*

20–22. Morning Prayer.

I thank Thee, my heavenly Father,
through Jesus Christ, Thy dear Son,
that Thou hast kept me this night from all harm
    and danger;
and I pray Thee
that Thou wouldst keep me this day also from
    sin and every evil,
that all my doings and life may please Thee.
For into Thy hands I commend myself,
my body and soul, and all things.
Let Thy holy angel be with me,
that the wicked Foe may have no power
    over me.   *Catechism, p. 22.*

23, 24. Evening Prayer.

I thank Thee, my heavenly Father,
through Jesus Christ, Thy dear Son,
that Thou hast graciously kept me this day;
and I pray Thee
that Thou wouldst forgive me all my sins
    where I have done wrong,
and graciously keep me this night.
For into Thy hands I commend myself,
my body and soul, and all things.
Let Thy holy angel be with me,
that the wicked Foe may have no power
    over me. Amen.   *Catechism, p. 23.*

25. *Review Lessons 20–24.*

Unit III — God's Word

26. *Review Grade II, Lessons 35, 36;*
    Grade III, Lessons 32, 33.

27. *Review Grade III, Lessons 35–37.*

28, 29. God's Word is true.

> **678.** The Word of the Lord is right;
> and all His works are done in truth.
> *Ps. 33:4.*

We must teach God's Word as God gives it to us.

> **445.** In vain they do worship Me, teaching for
> doctrines the commandments of men.
> *Matt. 15:9.*

We must obey all teachings of God's Word.

> **471.** Teaching them to observe all things what-
> soever I have commanded you.
> *Matt. 28:20.*

Unit IV — Catechism Review

30. *Review Grade III, Lessons 85–87.*
    (Commandments 1, 2.)

31. *Review Grade III, Lessons 88, 89.*
    (Commandment 3.)

32. *Review Grade III, Lessons 91, 92.*
    (Commandment 4.)

33. *Review Grade III, Lessons 85–92.*
    (Commandments 1–4.)

34. *Review Grade III, Lessons 93, 94.*
    (Commandment 5.)

35. *Review Grade III, Lessons 96, 97.*
(Commandment 6.)

36. *Review Grade III, Lessons 98, 99.*
(Commandment 7.)

37. *Review Grade III, Lessons 101, 102.*
(Commandment 8.)

38. *Review Grade III, Lessons 93–102.*
(Commandments 5–8.)

39. *Review Grade III, Lessons 103, 104.*
(Commandment 9.)

40. *Review Grade III, Lessons 106, 107.*
(Commandment 10.)

41, 42. *Review Grade III, Lessons 108–112.*
(Close of the Commandments.)

43. *Review Grade III, Lessons 103–112.*
(Commandment IX to Close.)

44–46. *Review Grade II, Lessons 42–49. (First Article.)*

47–49. *Review Grade II, Lessons 59–66. (Second Article.)*

Unit V — Salvation and Faith

50. *Review Grade I, Lessons 54–59;*
Grade II, Lessons 51–56.

51. *Review Grade III, Lessons 54–57.*

52. *Review Grade III, Lessons 59–63.*

53. We are saved alone by faith.

> 496. A man is justified by faith without the deeds of the Law. *Rom. 3:28.*

Our faith must rest in Christ.

> 469. Other foundation can no man lay than that is laid, which is Jesus Christ. *1 Cor. 3:11.*

54. We come to faith through hearing God's Word.

    234. How shall they believe in Him of whom they have not heard?   *Rom. 10:14.*

    235. So, then, faith cometh by hearing, and hearing by the Word of God. *Rom. 10:17.*

55. The Holy Ghost works faith.

    424. No man can say that Jesus is the Lord but by the Holy Ghost.   *1 Cor. 12:3.*

    450. He which hath begun a good work in you will perform it until the day of Jesus Christ.   *Phil. 1:6.*

56. *Review Lessons 53–55.*

57. The Holy Ghost works faith also through Baptism.

    626. Except a man be born of water and of the Spirit,

        he cannot enter into the kingdom of God; that which is born of the flesh is flesh. *John 3:5, 6.*

58. We must believe until we die.

    702. Be thou faithful unto death, and I will give thee a crown of life. *Rev. 2:10.*

    God keeps us in faith.

    449. Ye are kept by the power of God through faith unto salvation.   *1 Pet. 1:5.*

59. The believer is a new man.

   440. If any man be in Christ, he is a new creature.   *2 Cor. 5:17.*

   264. Put on the new man, which after God is created in righteousness and true holiness.   *Eph. 4:24.*

60. *Review Lessons 57–59.*

61. *Review Lessons 53–59.*

Unit VI — Third Article

62–66. The Third Article.

   I believe in the Holy Ghost; the holy Christian Church, the communion of saints; the forgiveness of sins; the resurrection of the body; and the life everlasting. Amen.

   What does this mean? I believe that I cannot by my own reason or strength believe in Jesus Christ, my Lord, or come to Him; but the Holy Ghost has called me by the Gospel, enlightened me with His gifts, sanctified and kept me in the true faith;

   even as He calls, gathers, enlightens, and sanctifies the whole Christian Church on earth, and keeps it with Jesus Christ in the one true faith;

   in which Christian Church He daily and richly forgives all sins to me and all believers,

   and will at the Last Day raise up me and all the dead, and give unto me and all believers in Christ eternal life.

   This is most certainly true.

Unit VII — Christmas

67. *Review Grade I, Lessons 61–73;*

    Grade II, Lessons 70–72.

68. *Review Grade III, Lessons 69–72.*

69. Jesus is the Son of God.

    310. Unto us a Child is born, unto us a Son is given;

    and the government shall be upon His shoulder;

    and His name shall be called Wonderful, Counselor,

    the Mighty God, the Everlasting Father, the Prince of Peace. *Is. 9:6.*

70. A Christmas Hymn.

    Silent night! Holy night!
    All is calm, all is bright,
    Round yon Virgin Mother and Child.
    Holy Infant, so tender and mild,
    Sleep in heavenly peace, sleep in heavenly
    peace. *L. H., 646:1.*

    Silent night! Holy night!
    Shepherds quake at the sight;
    Glories stream from heaven afar,
    Heavenly hosts sing, Alleluia,
    Christ, the Savior, is born! Christ, the Savior,
    is born! *L. H., 646:2.*

71. Silent night! Holy night!
   Son of God, love's pure light
   Radiant beams from Thy holy face,
   With the dawn of redeeming grace,
   Jesus, Lord, at Thy birth, Jesus, Lord,
       at Thy birth.   *L. H., 646:3.*

72. *Review Lessons 69–71.*

Unit VIII — Love

73. *Review Grade I, Lessons 77–81;*
   Grade II, Lessons 75, 76.

74. *Review Grade III, Lessons 76–79.*

75, 76. We should not judge unkindly.

179. Judge not, and ye shall not be judged;
       condemn not, and ye shall not be
           condemned.   *Luke 6:37.*

Love repays evil with good and may cause an enemy
to repent.

136. If thine enemy hunger, feed him;
       if he thirst, give him drink;
       for in so doing, thou shalt heap coals of
       fire on his head.   *Rom. 12:20.*

Unit IX — Trust

77. *Review Grade II, Lessons 78–84;*
   Grade III, Lessons 83, 84.

78. A Hymn of Trust.
   I am trusting Thee, Lord Jesus,
       Trusting only Thee;
   Trusting Thee for full salvation,
       Great and free.   *L. H., 428:1.*

I am trusting Thee for pardon;
  At Thy feet I bow,
For Thy grace and tender mercy
  Trusting now.   *L. H., 428:2.*

79. I am trusting Thee for cleansing
  In the crimson flood;
Trusting Thee to make me holy
  By Thy blood.   *L. H., 428:3.*

I am trusting Thee to guide me;
  Thou alone shalt lead,
Every day and hour supplying
  All my need.   *L. H., 428:4.*

80. *Review Lessons 78, 79.*

Unit X — The Sacrament of Holy Baptism (Fourth Chief Part)

81, 82. What is Baptism?

Baptism is not simple water only, but it is the water comprehended in God's command and connected with God's word.

Which is that word of God? (Review.)

Christ, our Lord, says in the last chapter of Matthew: Go ye and teach all nations, baptizing them in the name of the Father and of the Son and of the Holy Ghost.

83, 84. What does Baptism give or profit?

It works forgiveness of sins, delivers from death and the devil, and gives eternal salvation to all who believe this, as the words and promises of God declare.

Which are such words and promises of God? (Review.)
Christ, our Lord, says in the last chapter of
Mark: He that believeth and is baptized
shall be saved; but he that believeth not
shall be damned.

85–90. How can water do such great things?

It is not the water indeed that does them, but
the word of God which is in and with the
water, and faith, which trusts such word of
God in the water. For without the word of
God the water is simple water and no Baptism. But with the word of God it is a
Baptism, that is, a gracious water of life and
a washing of regeneration in the Holy Ghost,
as St. Paul says, Titus, chapter third:

According to His mercy He saved us by the
washing of regeneration and renewing of the
Holy Ghost, which He shed on us abundantly
through Jesus Christ, our Savior, that, being
justified by His grace, we should be made
heirs according to the hope of eternal life.
This is a faithful saying.

91–93. What does such baptizing with water signify?

It signifies that the Old Adam in us should, by
daily contrition and repentance, be drowned
and die with all sins and evil lusts and,
again, a new man daily come forth and arise,
who shall live before God in righteousness
and purity forever.

94, 95. Where is this written?

> St. Paul writes, Romans, chapter sixth: We are buried with Christ by Baptism into death, that, like as He was raised up from the dead by the glory of the Father, even so we also should walk in newness of life.

96. *Review Lessons 81–90.*

97. *Review Lessons 91–95.*

98. *Review Lessons 81–95.*

Unit XI — Prayer

99. Prayer before Meals.

> Lord God, heavenly Father,
> bless us and these Thy gifts
> which we receive from Thy bountiful goodness,
> through Jesus Christ, our Lord. Amen.
>
> *Catechism, p. 24.*

100. Prayer after Meals.

> For food and drink and happy days
> Accept our gratitude and praise;
> In serving others, Lord, may we,
> Repay in part our debt to Thee. Amen.

*101. Beginning of School Day.

> Lord Jesus Christ, be present now,
> Our hearts in true devotion bow,
> Thy Spirit send with grace divine,
> And let Thy truth within us shine.
>
> *L. H., 3:1.*

102. *Review Lessons 99–101.*

103. Prayer for the School.

Our Father, 'tis to Thee
We bring this earnest plea:
    God bless our school!
Thy saving Word is here;
Fill us with holy fear,
Make this a place most dear:
    God bless our school!

S. S., *127:1.*

104. Our Savior, from above
Guide with Thy tender love
    Our Lutheran school;
Help us our work to do,
And make us ever true;
Our number large or few:
    God bless our school!

S. S., *127:2.*

105. *Review Lessons 103, 104.*

*106. Before Leaving Church.

On what has now been sown
    Thy blessing, Lord, bestow;
The power is Thine alone
    To make it spring and grow.
Do Thou in grace the harvest raise,
And Thou alone shalt have the praise.

L. H., 46:1.

107. Hymn of Praise.

Now thank we all our God
    With heart and hands and voices,
Who wondrous things hath done,
    In whom His world rejoices;

Who from our mother's arms
    Hath blessed us on our way
With countless gifts of love,
    And still is ours today.   *L. H., 36:1.*

108. Oh, may this bounteous God
    Through all our life be near us,
With ever joyful hearts
    And blessed peace to cheer us
And keep us in His grace
    And guide us when perplexed
And free us from all ills
    In this world and the next!   *L. H., 36:2.*

109. *Review Lessons 107, 108.*

110. All praise and thanks to God
    The Father now be given,
The Son, and Him who reigns
    With them in highest heaven:
The one eternal God,
    Whom earth and heaven adore!
For thus it was, is now,
    And shall be evermore.   *L. H., 36:3.*

111. *Review Lessons 106–110.*

112. *Review Lessons 99–101.*

113. *Review Lessons 103–106.*

114. *Review Lessons 107–110.*

Unit XII — Obedience

115. *Review Grade I, Lessons 123, 124;*
Grade II, Lessons 96, 97;
Grade III, Lessons 140–145.

116. We must do the will of God from the heart.

92. Not every one that saith unto Me, Lord, Lord, shall enter into the kingdom of heaven;

but he that doeth the will of My Father which is in heaven.   *Matt. 7:21.*

Unit XIII — Death and Heaven

117. Christians want to be in heaven.

516. I have a desire to depart and to be with Christ,

which is far better.   *Phil. 1:23.*

In heaven there is only happiness.

520. In Thy presence is fullness of joy;

at Thy right hand there are pleasures forevermore.   *Ps. 16:11.*

Unit XIV — The Judgment

118. Jesus will judge the world.

397. He will judge the world in righteousness by that Man whom He hath ordained.   *Acts 17:31.*

It is too late to repent after death.

552. It is appointed unto men once to die, but after this the Judgment.   *Heb. 9:27.*

119. *Review Lessons 117, 118.*

Unit XV — Sin and Punishment

120. *Review Grade I, Lessons 127, 128;*
Grade II, Lessons 123–130.

121. *Review Grade III, Lessons 122–126.*

122. By nature we are altogether sinful.

> 221. I know that in me (that is, in my flesh) dwelleth no good thing. *Rom. 7:18.*

> 223. Ye were dead in trespasses and sins. *Eph. 2:1.*

123. We often sin without knowing it.

> 593. Who can understand his errors?
> Cleanse Thou me from secret faults. *Ps. 19:12.*

Sin makes us unworthy to be God's children.

> 596. Father, I have sinned against Heaven and in thy sight
> and am no more worthy to be called thy son. *Luke 15:21.*

124. *Review Lessons 122, 123.*

125. Cursing by God's name is sin.

> 78. Whosoever curseth his God shall bear his sin. *Lev. 24:15.*

False swearing is sin.

> 85. Ye shall not swear by My name falsely. *Lev. 19:12.*

126. Hatred is murder before God.

> **133.** Whosoever hateth his brother is
> a murderer;
> and ye know that no murderer hath eternal
> life abiding in him.   *1 John 3:15.*

God punishes the liar.

> **173.** A false witness shall not be unpunished.
> *Prov. 19:5.*

127. *Review Lessons 125, 126.*

128. *Review Lessons 122–126.*

Unit XVI — Forgiveness of Sins

129. We have forgiveness in Christ.
> Chief of sinners though I be,
> Jesus shed His blood for me;
> Died that I might live on high,
> Lived that I might never die.
> As the branch is to the vine,
> I am His, and He is mine.   *L. H., 342:1.*

130. Oh, the height of Jesus' love!
> Higher than the heavens above,
> Deeper than the depths of sea,
> Lasting as eternity.
> Love that found me — wondrous thought! —
> Found me when I sought Him not.
>   *L. H., 342:2.*

131. O my Savior, help afford
> By Thy Spirit and Thy Word!
> When my wayward heart would stray,
> Keep me in the narrow way;
> Grace in time of need supply
> While I live and when I die.   *L. H., 342:5.*

132. *Review Lessons 129–131.*

133. We should praise God for His forgiveness.

> **484.** Bless the Lord, O my soul, and forget not
> all His benefits;
>> who forgiveth all thine iniquities; who
>> healeth all thy diseases. *Ps. 103:2, 3.*

We must ask forgiveness from those whom we have wronged.

> **669.** Confess your faults one to another.
> *James 5:16.*

134. *Review Lessons 129–133.*

Unit XVII — Easter: The Resurrection

135. *Review Grade III, Lessons 135–137.*

> *Because Christ rose, our sins are forgiven.
> **380.** If Christ be not raised, your faith is vain;
> ye are yet in your sins. *1 Cor. 15:17.*

136. All believers will rise to eternal life.

> **383.** I am the Resurrection and the Life.
> He that believeth in Me, though he were
> dead, yet shall he live;
> and whosoever liveth and believeth in Me
> shall never die. *John 11:25, 26.*

Unit XVIII — The Sacrament
of the Altar (Sixth Chief Part)

137, 138. What is the Sacrament of the Altar?

> It is the true body and blood of our Lord Jesus
> Christ under the bread and wine, for us
> Christians to eat and to drink, instituted by
> Christ Himself.

139, 140. Where is this written?   (Review.)

> The holy Evangelists Matthew, Mark, Luke, and St. Paul [the Apostle] write thus:
>
> Our Lord Jesus Christ, the same night in which He was betrayed, took bread; and when He had given thanks, He brake it and gave it to His disciples, saying, Take, eat; this is My body, which is given for you. This do in remembrance of Me.
>
> After the same manner also He took the cup when He had supped, and when He had given thanks, He gave it to them, saying, Drink ye all of it; this cup is the new testament in My blood, which is shed for you for the remission of sins. This do, as oft as ye drink it, in remembrance of Me.

141, 142. What is the benefit of such eating and drinking?

> That is shown us by these words, "Given and shed for you for the remission of sins"; namely, that in the Sacrament forgiveness of sins, life, and salvation are given us through these words. For where there is forgiveness of sins, there is also life and salvation.

143. *Review Lessons 137–142.*

144, 145. How can bodily eating and drinking do such great things?

> It is not the eating and drinking indeed that does them, but the words here written, "Given and shed for you for the remission of sins"; which words, besides the bodily eating and drinking, are the chief thing in

the Sacrament; and he that believes these words has what they say and express, namely, the forgiveness of sins.

146, 147. Who, then, receives such Sacrament worthily?
Fasting and bodily preparation are indeed a fine outward training; but he is truly worthy and well prepared who has faith in these words, "Given and shed for you for the remission of sins."

But he that does not believe these words, or doubts, is unworthy and unprepared; for the words "for you" require all hearts to believe.

148. *Review Lessons 144–147.*

149. *Review Lessons 137–147.*

Unit XIX — Review

150. *Review Lessons 3, 4.*

151. *Review Lessons 6–8.*

152. *Review Lessons 17, 18.*

153. *Review Lessons 20–24.*

154. *Review Lessons 28, 29.*

155. *Review Lessons 53–55.*

156. *Review Lessons 57–59.*

157. *Review Lessons 62–66.*

158. *Review Lessons 69–71.*

159. *Review Lessons 75, 76, 78, 79.*

160. *Review Lessons 81–90.*

161. *Review Lessons 91–95.*

162. *Review Lessons 81–95.*

163. *Review Lessons 99–101.*

164. *Review Lessons 103–106.*

165. *Review Lessons 107–110.*

Unit XX — The Ascension

166. Christ ascended to heaven.

> [392.] This same Jesus which is taken up from
> you into heaven
>   shall so come in like manner as ye have
>   seen Him go into heaven. *Acts 1:11.*

167. An Ascension Hymn.
Draw us to Thee,
For then shall we
  Walk in Thy steps forever
And hasten on
Where Thou art gone
  To be with Thee, dear Savior.

L. H., 215:1.

168. Draw us to Thee,
Lord, lovingly;
  Let us depart with gladness
That we may be
Forever free
  From sorrow, grief, and sadness.

L. H., 215:2.

169. Draw us to Thee
Unceasingly,
  Into Thy kingdom take us;
Let us fore'er
Thy glory share,
  Thy saints and joint heirs make us.

L. H., 215:5.

170. *Review of Lessons 166–170.*

Unit XXI — Review

171. *Review Lessons 116–118.*

172. *Review Lessons 122, 123.*

173. *Review Lessons 125, 126.*

174. *Review Lessons 129–131.*

175. *Review Lessons 129–133.*

176. *Review Lesson 136.*

177. *Review Lessons 137–142.*

178. *Review Lessons 144–147.*

179. *Review Lessons 137–147.*

180. *Review Lessons 166–169.*

Grade 5

Unit I — God

LESSONS

1. *Review Grade II, Lessons 2—6;*
   Grade III, Lessons 3, 4.

2. *Review Grade III, Lessons 6, 7;*
   Grade IV, Lessons 3, 4.

3. *Review Grade IV, Lessons 6—8.*

4. All men should fear God.

   65. Let all the earth fear the Lord. . . .
       Ps. 33:8.

   82. Thou shalt fear the Lord, thy God. . . .
       Deut. 6:13.

5. God will not give up His glory.

   55. I am the Lord; that is My name. . . .
       Is. 42:8.

   Jesus is God with the Father.

   309. In Him dwelleth all the fullness. . . .
       Col. 2:9.

6. *Review Lessons 4, 5.*

Unit II — God's Word

7. *Review Grade II, Lessons 35, 36;*
   Grade III, Lessons 32, 33.

8. *Review Grade III, Lessons 35—37;*
   Grade IV, Lessons 28, 29.

9. God's Word is inspired.

> 1. Holy men of God spake. . . . *2 Peter 1:21.*

God's Word shows us the way to eternal life.

> 10. Search the Scriptures. . . . *John 5:39.*

10. We should love God's Word.

> 16. These words which I command thee. . . .
> *Deut. 6:6, 7.*

God speaks through Christian pastors.

> 104. He that heareth you heareth Me. . . .
> *Luke 10:16.*

11. Attendance at public worship is a Christian duty.

> *101. Not forsaking the assembling. . . .
> *Heb. 10:25.*

> 102. They continued steadfastly. . . . *Acts 2:42.*

12. *Review Lessons 9–11.*

Unit III — Prayer

13. *Review Grade II, Lessons 16–31.*
14. *Review Grade II, Lessons 99–114.*
15. *Review Grade III, Lessons 17–21.*
16. *Review Grade III, Lessons 23–27.*
17. *Review Grade IV, Lessons 17–24; 99–101.*
18. *Review Grade IV, Lessons 103–110.*
19. Prayer before Meals.

> Grant us grace, O Lord,
> that whether we eat or drink,
> or whatsoever we do,
> we may do it all in Thy name
> and to Thy glory. Amen.   *L. F. H., 47.*

Prayer after Meals.

Bless the Lord, O my soul;
and all that is within me, bless His holy name.
Bless the Lord, O my soul,
And forget not all His benefits. Amen.
    Ps. 103:1, 2.

20. *Upon Entering Church.

Distracting thoughts and cares remove
And fix our hearts and hopes above;
With food divine may we be fed
And satisfied with living bread.

                                    H. B., 4:2.

Before Leaving Church.

Now the blessing cheers our heart,
    By His grace to us extended.
Let us joyfully depart;
    Be our souls to God commended.
May His Spirit ever guide us
And with all good gifts provide us.

                                    L. H., 45:2.

21. *Review Lessons 19, 20.*

22. Prayer for Obedience to Parents.

O God, I thank Thee heartily
That Thou dear parents gavest me,
    A gift of love so tender,
That they might be a joy to me —
    For this glad praise I render.

                                    Kg., 335:1.

23. My heart with glad obedience fill
 That joyfully I do their will
  And duty be my pleasure.
 Help me, O Lord, that I regard
  Them as a precious treasure. G., 335:2.

24. *Review Lessons 19–23.*

25. A Prayer of Praise.
 The Lord hath helped me hitherto
  By His surpassing favor;
 His mercies every morn were new,
  His kindness did not waver.
 God hitherto hath been my Guide,
 Hath pleasures hitherto supplied,
 And hitherto hath helped me. L. H., 33:1.

26. I praise and thank Thee, Lord, my God,
  For Thine abundant blessing
 Which heretofore Thou hast bestowed
  And I am still possessing.
 Inscribe this on my memory:
 The Lord hath done great things for me
 And graciously hath helped me. L. H., 33:2.

27. Help me henceforth, O God of grace,
  Help me on each occasion,
 Help me in each and every place,
  Help me through Jesus' Passion;
 Help me in life and death, O God,
 Help me through Jesus' dying blood;
 Help me as Thou hast helped me.
        L. H., 33:3.

28. *Review Lessons 25–27.*

29. *Review Lessons 19–27.*

Unit IV — The Reformation

30. A Reformation Hymn.

A mighty Fortress is our God,
　A trusty Shield and Weapon;
He helps us free from every need
　That hath us now o'ertaken.
The old evil Foe
Now means deadly woe;
Deep guile and great might
Are his dread arms in fight;
　On earth is not his equal.   *L. H., 262:1.*

31. With might of ours can naught be done,
　Soon were our loss effected;
But for us fights the Valiant One,
　Whom God Himself elected.
Ask ye, Who is this?
Jesus Christ it is,
Of Sabaoth Lord,
And there's none other God;
　He holds the field forever.   *L. H., 262:2.*

32. *Review Lessons 30, 31.*

33. Though devils all the world should fill,
　All eager to devour us,
We tremble not, we fear no ill,
　They shall not overpower us.
This world's prince may still
Scowl fierce as he will,
He can harm us none,
He's judged; the deed is done;
　One little word can fell him.   *L. H., 262:3.*

34. The Word they still shall let remain
     Nor any thanks have for it;
He's by our side upon the plain
     With His good gifts and Spirit.
And take they our life,
Good's, fame, child, and wife,
Let these all be gone,
They yet have nothing won;
     The Kingdom ours remaineth. *L. H., 262:4.*

35. *Review Lessons 33, 34.*

36. *Review Lessons 30–34.*

Unit V — Catechism Review (First and Second Chief Parts)

37. *Review Commandments 1, 2.*

38. *Review Commandments 3, 4.*

39. *Review Commandments 1–4.*

40. *Review Commandments 5, 6.*

41. *Review Commandments 7, 8.*

42. *Review Commandments 5–8.*

43. *Review Commandments 9, 10.*

44. *Review Close of Commandments.*

45. *Review Commandment 9 to Close.*

46. *Review entire First Chief Part (the Ten Commandments).*

47. *Review First Article.*

48. *Review Second Article.*

49. *Review Third Article.*

50. *Review entire Second Chief Part (the Creed).*

Unit VI — Salvation and Faith

51. *Review Grade II, Lessons 51–56.*
   Grade III, Lessons 54–57.

52. *Review Grade III, Lessons 59–63.*

53. *Review Grade IV, Lessons 53–55.*

54. *Review Grade IV, Lessons 57–59.*

55. We are saved by grace, through faith.
   423. By grace are ye saved. . . . *Eph. 2:8, 9.*
   561. Ye are all the children of God. . . .
   Gal. 3:26.

56.*We have eternal life in Christ.
   358. Our Savior, Jesus Christ, hath abolished
   death. . . . *2 Tim. 1:10.*
   Salvation is possible only through Jesus.
   282. Neither is there salvation in any other. . . .
   Acts 4:12.

57. *Review Lessons 55, 56.*

58.*Faith is a matter of the heart.
   461. The kingdom of God cometh not with
   observation. . . . *Luke 17:20, 21.*
   We must often examine ourselves.
   474. Examine yourselves. . . . *2 Cor. 13:5.*
   The Christian is beset with troubles.
   609. We must through much tribulation. . . .
   Acts 14:22.

59. The devil tries to destroy our faith.
   260. Be sober, be vigilant. . . . *1 Peter 5:8, 9.*
   God sent Jesus to destroy the power of the devil.

359. I will put enmity between thee and the woman. . . . *Gen. 3:15.*

60. *Review Lessons 58, 59.*

61. *Review Lessons 55–59.*

Unit VII — Catechism Review (Fourth and Sixth Chief Parts)

62. The Sacrament of Holy Baptism.
    What is Baptism?
    Which is that word of God?
    What does Baptism give or profit?
    Which are such words and promises of God?

63. How can water do such great things?

64. What does such baptizing with water signify?
    Where is this written?

65. *Review entire Fourth Chief Part*
    (the Sacrament of Holy Baptism).

66. The Sacrament of the Altar.
    What is the Sacrament of the Altar?
    Where is this written?

67. What is the benefit of such eating and drinking?

68. How can bodily eating and drinking do such great things?

69. Who, then, receives such Sacrament worthily?

70. *Review entire Sixth Chief Part*
    (the Sacrament of the Altar).

Unit VIII — Advent and Christmas

71. *Review Grade II, Lessons 70–72.*
Grade III, Lessons 69–72.

72. *Review Grade IV, Lessons 69–71.*

73. An Advent Prayer.
Come, Thou precious Ransom, come,
    Only Hope for sinful mortals!
Come, O Savior of the world!
    Open are to Thee all portals.
Come, Thy beauty let us see;
Anxiously we wait for Thee.   *L. H., 55:1.*

74. Enter now my waiting heart,
    Glorious King and Lord most holy.
Dwell in me and ne'er depart,
    Though I am but poor and lowly.
Ah, what riches will be mine
When Thou art my Guest Divine!
                                        L. H., 55:2.
75. *Review Lessons 73, 74.*

Unit IX — Love

76. *Review Grade II, Lessons 75, 76;*
Grade III, Lessons 75, 76.

77. *Review Grade III, Lessons 76–79.*

78. God loved us enough to make us His children.

[558.] Behold what manner of love. . . .
    1 John 3:1.

*Love helps us to overlook faults.

[184.] Charity believeth all things. . . . *1 Cor. 13:7.*

79. We should treat others as we want to be treated.

   118. All things whatsoever ye would. . . . *Matt. 7:12.*

   We should honor the aged.

   122. Thou shalt rise up. . . . *Lev. 19:32.*

80. *Review Lessons 78, 79.*

81. God rewards love.

   137. Blessed are the meek. . . . *Matt. 5:5, 7, 9.*

   170. He that hath pity. . . . *Prov. 19:17.*

   *171. To do good and to communicate. . . . *Heb. 13:16.*

82. *Review Lessons 78–81.*

Unit X — Trust

83. *Review Grade II, Lessons 78–84; Grade III, Lessons 83, 84.*

84. *Review Grade IV, Lessons 78, 79.*

Unit XI — The Lord's Prayer with Explanation (Third Chief Part)

85. The Introduction.

86, 87. The First Petition.

88, 89. The Second Petition.

   90. *Review Lessons 85–89. Introduction to Second Petition.*

91, 92. The Third Petition.

93, 94. The Fourth Petition.

95, 96. The Fifth Petition.

97. *Review Lessons 91–96. Third to Fifth Petitions.*

98. The Sixth Petition.

99. The Seventh Petition.

100. The Conclusion.

101. *Review Lessons 98–100. Sixth Petition to Conclusion.*

102. *Review Lessons 85–89. Introduction to Second Petition.*

103. *Review Lessons 91–96. Third to Fifth Petitions.*

104. *Review Lessons 98–100. Sixth Petition to Conclusion.*

105. *Review entire Third Chief Part.*

Unit XII — The Judgment

106. *Review Grade IV, Lesson 118.*

107. Judgment Day will surely come.

[506.] The hour is coming. . . . *John 5:28, 29.*

No man knows the Day of Judgment.

[400.] Of that day and that hour knoweth no man. . . . *Mark 13:32.*

Unit XIII — The Sacraments

108. Self-examination is necessary before partaking of the Lord's Supper.

[699.] Let a man examine himself. . . . *1 Cor. 11:28.*

Unit XIV — Cross and Comfort

109. God invites the sinner and comforts him.

[691.] Come unto Me. . . . *Matt. 11:28.*

A Hymn of Comfort.

If thou but suffer God to guide thee
    And hope in Him through all thy ways,
He'll give thee strength, whate'er betide thee,
    And bear thee through the evil days.
Who trusts in God's unchanging love
Builds on the Rock that naught can move.

L. H., 518:1.

110. What can these anxious cares avail thee,
    These never-ceasing moans and sighs?
What can it help if thou bewail thee
    O'er each dark moment as it flies?
Our cross and trials do but press
The heavier for our bitterness.   *L. H., 518:2.*

111. *Review Lessons 109, 110.*

*112. Be patient and await His leisure
    In cheerful hope, with heart content
To take whate'er Thy Father's pleasure
    And His discerning love hath sent,
Nor doubt our inmost wants are known
To Him who chose us for His own.

L. H., 518:3.

113. Sing, pray, and keep His ways unswerving,
    Perform thy duties faithfully,
And trust His Word; though undeserving,
    Thou yet shalt find it true for thee.
God never yet forsook in need
The soul that trusted Him indeed.

L. H., 518:7.

114. *Review Lessons 109–113.*

Unit XV — Sin and Punishment

115. *Review Grade II, Lessons 123–130;*
   Grade III, Lessons 122–126.

116. *Review Grade IV, Lessons 122–126.*

117. All are sinners.
   205. We are all as an unclean thing. . . .
      Is. 64:6.

   208. If we say that we have no sin. . . .
      1 John 1:8.

118. Misuse of God's name is sin.
   77. The Lord will not hold him guiltless. . . .
      Ex. 20:7.

   Swearing in unimportant matters is sin.
   84. Let your communication be, Yea, yea. . . .
      Matt. 5:37.

119. *Review Lessons 117, 118.*

120. Gossip is sin.
   176. A talebearer revealeth secrets. . . .
      Prov. 11:13.

   God punishes the murderer.
   128. Whoso sheddeth man's blood. . . .
      Gen. 9:6.

121. We must avoid secret sins.
   148. It is a shame even to speak. . . . *Eph. 5:12.*
   We must not spread the sins of others.
   180. If thy brother shall trespass. . . .
      Matt. 18:15.

122. *Review Lessons 117–121.*

Unit XVI — The Angels

123. *Review Grade III, Lesson 119.*
     The angels serve the believers.

     248. Are they not all ministering spirits. . . .
          Heb. 1:14.

Unit XVII — Forgiveness of Sins

124. *Review Grade IV, Lessons 129–133.*

125. We have forgiveness in Christ.

     351. He hath made Him to be sin for us. . . .
          2 Cor. 5:21.

     We must confess our sins.

     664. He that covereth his sins. . . . *Prov. 28:13.*

126. Christ receives sinners.
     Jesus sinners doth receive;
        Oh, may all this saying ponder
     Who in sin's delusions live
        And from God and heaven wander!
     Here is hope for all who grieve —
     Jesus sinners doth receive.   *L. H., 324:1.*

127. We deserve but grief and shame;
        Yet His words, rich grace revealing,
     Pardon, peace, and life proclaim.
        Here their ills have perfect healing
     Who with humble hearts believe —
     Jesus sinners doth receive.   *L. H., 324:2.*

*128. Sheep that from the fold did stray
    No true shepherd e'er forsaketh;
Weary souls that lost their way
    Christ, the Shepherd, gently taketh
In His arms that they may live —
Jesus sinners doth receive.   *L. H., 324:3.*

129. Come, ye sinners, one and all,
    Come, accept His invitation;
Come, obey His gracious call,
    Come and take His free salvation!
Firmly in these words believe:
Jesus sinners doth receive.   *L. H., 324:4.*

130. *Review Lessons 125–129.*

Unit XVIII — The Passion

131. *Review Grade II, Lessons 135–137.*
132. *Review Grade III, Lessons 130–133.*

Unit XIX — Easter: The Resurrection

133. *Review Grade III, Lessons 135–137;
Grade IV, Lesson 136.*

134. We shall rise in the likeness of God.

    266. I will behold Thy face in righteousness. . . .
      Ps. 17:15.

135. An Easter Hymn.
Jesus Christ, my sure Defense
    And my Savior, ever liveth;
Knowing this, my confidence
    Rests upon the hope it giveth
Though the night of death be fraught
Still with many an anxious thought.
     L. H., 206:1.

136. Jesus, my Redeemer, lives;
    I, too, unto life shall waken.
  Endless joy my Savior gives;
    Shall my courage, then, be shaken?
  Shall I fear, or could the Head
  Rise and leave His members dead?

L. H., 206:2.

137. Glorified, I shall anew
    With this flesh then be enshrouded;
  In this body I shall view
    God, my Lord, with eyes unclouded;
  In this flesh I then shall see
  Jesus Christ eternally.   *L. H., 206:5.*

138. *Review Lessons 134–137.*

Unit XX — Death and Heaven

139. *Review Grade IV, Lesson 117.*
  The Christian looks with joy toward heaven.

    614. Lord, now lettest Thou Thy servant. . . .
      Luke 2:29, 30.

140. Prayer for a Peaceful Death.
  My Savior, be Thou near me
    When death is at my door;
  Then let Thy presence cheer me,
    Forsake me nevermore!
  When soul and body languish,
    Oh, leave me not alone,
  But take away mine anguish
    By virtue of Thine own!   *L. H., 172:9.*

141. Be Thou my Consolation
    My Shield, when I must die;
Remind me of Thy Passion
    When my last hour draws nigh.
Mine eyes shall then behold Thee,
    Upon Thy cross shall dwell,
My heart by faith enfold Thee.
    Who dieth thus dies well.   *L. H., 172:10.*

142. *Review Lessons 139–141.*

Unit XXI — The Office of the Keys and Confession (Fifth Chief Part)

143. What is the Office of the Keys?

144. Where is this written?

145, 146. What do you believe according to these words?

147. *Review Lessons 143–146.*

148. What is Confession?

149. What sins should we confess?

150. Which are these?

151. *Review Lessons 148–150.*

152. *Review Lessons 143–150. Entire Fifth Chief Part.*

Unit XXII — Review

153. *Review Lessons 4, 5, 73, 74.*

154. *Review Lessons 9–11.*

155. *Review Lessons 19–23.*

156. *Review Lessons 25–27.*

157. *Review Lessons 30–34.*

158. *Review Lessons 55–59.*

159. *Review Lessons 78–81.*

160. *Review Lessons 85–89.   Introduction to Second Petition.*

161. *Review Lessons 91–96.   Third to Fifth Petitions.*

162. *Review Lessons 98–100.   Sixth Petition to Conclusion.*

163. *Review Lessons 85–100.   Entire Third Chief Part.*

164. *Review Lessons 107, 108, 123.*

Unit XXIII — The Ascension

165. *Review Grade IV, Lessons 166–169.*

Unit XXIV — Obedience

166. *Review Grade II, Lessons 96, 97;
Grade III, Lessons 140–145; Grade IV, Lesson 116.*

167. God warns us against the broad way of unbelief.

515. Enter ye in at the strait gate. . . .
Matt. 7:13.

We should show in all we do that we are Christians.

447. Whether therefore ye eat or drink. . . .
1 Cor. 10:31.

168. Parents should bring up their children in the fear of God.

622. Ye fathers, provoke not your children. . . .
Eph. 6:4.

God promises blessings to obedient children.

121. Honor thy father and mother. . . .
Eph. 6:2, 3.

169. We must obey the government.
81. Let every soul be subject. . . . Rom. 13:1.
Obedient children of God are content.
590. Having food and raiment. . . . 1 Tim. 6:8.

170. Review Lessons 167–169.

Unit XXV — Pentecost; Mission Work

171. Review Grade III, Lessons 169–173.

172. The Christian must preach God's Word.
619. All power is given unto Me. . . .
Matt. 28:18–20.
We should pray for missions and missionaries.
569. Pray ye therefore the Lord. . . . Matt. 9:38.

Unit XXVI — Review

173. Review Lessons 109–113.

174. Review Lessons 117–121.

175. Review Lessons 125–129.

176. Review Lessons 134–137.

177. Review Lessons 139–141, 172.

178. Review Lessons 143–146. Office of the Keys, three questions.

179. Review Lessons 148–150. Confession, three questions.

180. Review Lessons 167–169.

MEMORY SELECTIONS

Grade 6

Unit I — God

1. *Review Grade III, Lessons 3–7;*
   Grade IV, Lessons 3, 4.

2. *Review Grade IV, Lessons 6–8;*
   Grade V, Lessons 4, 5.

3. Nature tells us there is a God.

   23. The heavens declare the glory of God. . . .
       Ps. 19:1.

   God is almighty.

   56. Our God is in the heavens. . . .
       Ps. 115:3, 4.

   *The Holy Ghost is omniscient.

   414. The Spirit searcheth all things. . . .
        1 Cor. 2:10.

4. We must fear God more than anyone else.

   58. Fear not them which kill the body. . . .
       Matt. 10:28.

   We must love God more than anyone else.

   59. He that loveth father or mother more
       than Me. . . . *Matt. 10:37.*

5. *Review Lessons 3, 4.*

6. God preserves and protects us.

   268. O Lord, Thou preservest. . . . *Ps. 36:6.*

115

273. There shall no evil befall thee. . . .
     Ps. 91:10.

God cares for us even in little things.

272. Are not two sparrows sold. . . .
     Matt. 10:29, 30.

7. *Review Lessons 3–6.*

Unit II — God's Word

8. *Review Grade III, Lessons 32–37;*
   Grade IV, Lessons 28, 29.

9. *Review Grade V, Lessons 9–11.*

10. God's Word is truth.

   105. When ye received the Word. . . .
        1 Thess. 2:13.

   °God warns against false prophets.

   89. Behold, I am against the prophets. . . .
       Jer. 23:31.

11. More warnings against false prophets.

   480. Beware of false prophets. . . . *Matt. 7:15.*

   481. Beloved, believe not every spirit. . . .
        John 4:1.

12. *Review Lessons 10, 11.*

Unit III — Prayer

13. *Review Grade III, Lessons 17–27.*

14. *Review Grade IV, Lessons 17–24; 99–101.*

15. *Review Grade IV, Lessons 103–110.*

16. *Review Grade V, Lessons 19–23.*

17. *Review Grade V, Lessons 19–27.*

18. God hears our prayers.

536. Ask, and it shall be given you. . . .
     Matt. 7:7, 8.

539. What things soever ye desire. . . .
     Mark 11:24.

19. We should pray for our enemies.

551. Pray for them which despitefully use. . . .
     Matt. 5:44.

Prayer before Meals.
Thy goodness let us trust, O Lord,
As promised in Thy changeless Word;
From sinful worry and from care
Keep Thou us here and everywhere.

20. Prayer after Meals.   *A. C. S., 55.*
Oh, give thanks unto the Lord. . . .

21. Prayer for Our Country.   *Catechism, p. 24.*
God bless our native land!
Firm may she ever stand
    Through storm and night!
When the wild tempests rave,
Ruler of wind and wave,
Do Thou our country save
    By Thy great might.   *L. H., 577:1.*

For her our prayer shall rise
To God above the skies;
    On Him we wait.
Thou who art ever nigh,
Guarding with watchful eye,
To Thee aloud we cry,
    God save the State!   *L. H., 577:2.*

22. *Review Lessons 18–21.*

23. Song of Praise.
> We sing the almighty power of God,
>> Who bade the mountains rise,
>
> Who spread the flowing seas abroad
>> And built the lofty skies.   *L. H., 43:1.*
>
> We sing the wisdom that ordained
>> The sun to rule the day;
>
> The moon shines, too, at His command,
>> And all the stars obey.   *L. H., 43:2.*

24. We sing the goodness of the Lord,
>> Who fills the earth with food,
>
> Who formed His creatures by a word
>> And then pronounced them good.
>>> *L. H., 43:3.*
>
> Lord, how Thy wonders are displayed
>> Where'er we turn our eyes,
>
> Whene'er we view the ground we tread
>> Or gaze upon the skies!   *L. H., 43:4.*

25. *Review Lessons 23, 24.*

26. *Review Lessons 18–24.*

Unit IV — Obedience

27. *Review Grade III, Lessons 140–145.*

28. *Review Grade IV, Lesson 116;*
Grade V, Lessons 167–169.

29. We must repay our parents.
> 123. Let them learn first to show piety. . . .
>> *1 Tim. 5:4.*
>
> God punishes disobedient children.

119. The eye that mocketh at his father. . . .
   Prov. 30:17.

30. Prayer for Obedience.
   Oh, that the Lord would guide my ways
      To keep His statutes still!
   Oh, that my God would grant me grace
      To know and do His will!   *L. H., 416:1.*

   Order my footsteps by Thy Word
      And make my heart sincere;
   Let sin have no dominion, Lord,
      But keep my conscience clear. *L. H., 416:2.*

31. Assist my soul, too apt to stray,
      A stricter watch to keep;
   And should I e'er forget Thy way,
      Restore Thy wandering sheep. *L. H., 416:3.*

   Make me to walk in Thy commands —
      'Tis a delightful road —
   Nor let my head or heart or hands
      Offend against my God.   *L. H., 416:4.*

32. *Review Lessons 29–31.*

Unit V — Reformation

33. *Review Grade V, Lessons 30, 31.* *L. H., 262:1, 2.*
34. *Review Grade V, Lessons 33, 34.* *L. H., 262:3, 4.*
35. *Review Grade V, Lessons 30–34.* *L. H., 262:1–4.*

Unit VI — Catechism Review
   First Chief Part.

36. *Commandments 1–3.*
37. *Commandments 4–6.*
38. *Commandments 7–9.*

39. *Commandment 10, Close of Commandments.*
40. *Commandments 1–6.*
41. *Commandment 7 to Close.*
42. *Entire First Chief Part.*
    Second Chief Part.
43. *First Article.*
44. *Second Article.*
45. *Third Article.*
46. *Entire Second Chief Part.*
    Third Chief Part.
47. *Introduction to Second Petition.*
48. *Third and Fourth Petitions.*
49. *Fifth and Sixth Petitions.*
50. *Seventh Petition, Conclusion.*
51. *Introduction to Fourth Petition.*
52. *Fifth Petition to Conclusion.*
53. *Entire Third Chief Part.*

Unit VII — Salvation and Faith

54. *Review Grade III, Lessons 54–63.*
55. *Review Grade IV, Lessons 53–59.*
56. *Review Grade V, Lessons 55, 56.*
57. *Review Grade V, Lessons 58, 59.*
58. We have salvation in Christ.
    320. Christ hath abolished death.
        2 Tim. 1:10.
    340. Though He was rich. . . . 2 Cor. 8:9.
    * 28. This is life eternal. . . . John 17:3.

59. God wants to save all people.

> 452. As I live, saith the Lord. . . . *Ezek. 33:11.*
> The Lord knows His children.
> 462. The foundation of God standeth. . . .
>   *2 Tim. 2:19.*

60. The Holy Ghost works faith.

> 419. But ye are washed. . . . *1 Cor. 6:11.*
> 460. If any man have not the Spirit. . . .
>   *Rom. 8:9.*

61. *Review Lessons 58–60.*

62, 63. Song of Faith in the Triune God.

> We all believe in one true God,
>   Father, Son, and Holy Ghost,
> Ever-present Help in need,
>   Praised by all the heavenly host,
> By whose mighty power alone
> All is made and wrought and done.   *L. H., 252:1.*
>
> We all believe in Jesus Christ,
>   Son of God and Mary's Son,
> Who descended from His throne
>   And for us salvation won;
> By whose cross and death are we
> Rescued from all misery.   *L. H., 252:2.*
>
> We all confess the Holy Ghost,
>   Who from both fore'er proceeds;
> Who upholds and comforts us
>   In all trials, fears, and needs.
> Blest and Holy Trinity,
> Praise forever be to Thee.   *L. H., 252:3.*

64. *Review Lessons 58–63.*

Unit VIII — Catechism Review

65. Fourth Chief Part.
    What is Baptism?
    Which is that word of God?
    What does Baptism give or profit?
    Which are such words and promises of God?

66. How can water do such great things?

67. What does such baptizing with water signify?
    Where is this written?

68. *Review entire Fourth Chief Part.*

Unit IX — Advent and Christmas

69. *Review Grade III, Lessons 69–72.*

70. *Review Grade IV, Lessons 69–71.*

71. *Review Grade V, Lessons 73, 74.*

72. An Advent Hymn.
    Lift up your heads, ye mighty gates!
    Behold, the King of Glory waits;
    The King of kings is drawing near,
    The Savior of the world is here.
    Life and salvation He doth bring,
    Wherefore rejoice and gladly sing:
    　　We praise Thee, Father, now,
    　　Creator, wise art Thou!　　*L. H., 73:1.*

*73. A Helper just He comes to Thee,
    His chariot is humility,
    His kingly crown is holiness,
    His scepter, pity in distress.
    The end of all our woe He brings;
    Wherefore the earth is glad and sings:
    　　We praise Thee, Savior, now,
    　　Mighty in deed art Thou!　　*L. H., 73:2.*

74. Redeemer, come! I open wide
    My heart to Thee; here, Lord, abide!
    Let me Thy inner presence feel,
    Thy grace and love in me reveal;
    Thy Holy Spirit guide us on
    Until our glorious goal is won.
        Eternal praise and fame
        We offer to Thy name.   *L. H.*, 73:5.

75. *Review Lessons 72–74.*

Unit X — Love

76. *Review Grade III, Lessons 76–79;
    Grade IV, Lessons 75, 76.*

77. *Review Grade V, Lessons 78–81.*

78. We love God, our only Helper.

    70. Whom have I in heaven. . . .
        Ps. 73:25, 26.

    God blesses those who love Him.

    194. Delight thyself also in the Lord. . . .
        Ps. 37:4.

79. We are to do good to all, especially our fellow
    Christians.

    116. As we have therefore opportunity. . . .
        Gal. 6:10.

    We should defend our neighbor in his absence.

    182. Open thy mouth for the dumb. . . .
        Prov. 31:8, 9.

80. *Review Lessons 78, 79.*

Unit XI — Trust

81. *Review Grade III, Lessons 83, 84;*
    Grade IV, Lessons 78, 79.

82. A Psalm of Trust.
    Psalm 23:1-3.

83. Psalm 23:4-6.

84. *Review Lessons 82, 83.   Psalm 23:1–6.*

Unit XII — Catechism Review

85. Fifth Chief Part.
    What is the Office of the Keys?
    Where is this written?

86. What do you believe according to these
    words?

87. What is Confession?
    What sins should we confess?

88. Which are these?

89. *Review entire Fifth Chief Part.*

90. Sixth Chief Part.
    What is the Sacrament of the Altar?
    Where is this written?

91. What is the benefit of such eating and
    drinking?

92. How can bodily eating and drinking do such
    great things?
    Who, then, receives such Sacrament worthily?

93. *Review entire Sixth Chief Part.*

Unit XIII — Table of Duties

94. What the Hearers Owe to Their Pastors.
    First *three* paragraphs.

95. *Fourth* paragraph.

96. *Fifth* paragraph.

97. *Sixth* paragraph.

98. *Review Lessons 94–97.*

99. Of Civil Government.
    Let every soul . . . to themselves damnation.

100. To Husbands.

101. To Wives.

102. To Parents; To Children; To All in Common.

103. *Review Lessons 99–102.*

104. *Review Lessons 94–97.*

105. *Review Lessons 94–102.*

Unit XIV — Christ's Office

106. Christ is our Prophet.
     323. The Lord, thy God, will raise up. . . .
     Deut. 18:15.

Unit XV — Cross and Comfort

107. *Review Grade V, Lessons 109, 110.*

108. *Review Grade V, Lessons 109–113.*

109. Christians must expect crosses.
     610. Whom the Lord loveth. . . . *Heb. 12:6.*
     God promises to help us bear our crosses.

611. My grace is sufficient. . . . *2 Cor. 12:9.*
God promises to remove our crosses.
612. He shall deliver thee. . . . *Job 5:19.*

110. A Hymn of Comfort.
What a Friend we have in Jesus,
  All our sins and griefs to bear!
What a privilege to carry
  Everything to God in prayer!
Oh, what peace we often forfeit,
  Oh, what needless pain we bear,
All because we do not carry
  Everything to God in prayer! *L. H., 457:1.*

111. Have we trials and temptations?
  Is there trouble anywhere?
We should never be discouraged,
  Take it to the Lord in prayer.
Can we find a Friend so faithful
  Who will all our sorrows share?
Jesus knows our every weakness —
  Take it to the Lord in prayer. *L. H., 457:2.*

112. Are we weak and heavy laden,
  Cumbered with a load of care?
Precious Savior, still our Refuge —
  Take it to the Lord in prayer.
Do thy friends despise, forsake thee?
  Take it to the Lord in prayer,
In His arms He'll take and shield thee,
  Thou wilt find a solace there. *L. H., 457:3.*

113. *Review Lessons 109–112.*

114. A Hymn of Comfort.

> The will of God is always best
>   And shall be done forever;
> And they who trust in Him are blest,
>   He will forsake them never.
> He helps indeed in time of need,
>   He chastens with forbearing;
> They who depend On God, their Friend,
>   Shall not be left despairing.   *L. H., 517:1.*

115. God is my Comfort and my Trust,
>   My Hope and Life abiding;
> And to His counsel, wise and just,
>   I yield, in Him confiding.
> The very hairs, His Word declares,
>   Upon my head He numbers.
> By night and day God is my Stay,
>   He never sleeps nor slumbers.   *L. H., 517:2.*

116. Lord Jesus, this I ask of Thee,
>   Deny me not this favor:
> When Satan sorely troubles me,
>   Then do not let me waver.
> Keep watch and ward, O gracious Lord,
>   Fulfill Thy faithful saying:
> Who doth believe, He shall receive
>   An answer to his praying.   *L. H., 517:3.*

117. When life's brief course on earth is run
>   And I this world am leaving,
> Grant me to say: "Thy will be done,"
>   By faith to Thee still cleaving.
> My heavenly Friend, I now commend
>   My soul into Thy keeping,

O'er sin and hell, And death as well,
Through Thee the victory reaping.

118. *Review Lessons 114–117.*   *L. H., 517:4.*

*119. A Hymn of Comfort.

How firm a foundation, ye saints of the Lord,
Is laid for your faith in His excellent Word!
What more can He say than to you He
    hath said
Who unto the Savior for refuge have fled?
                        L. H., 427:1.

In every condition — in sickness, in health,
In poverty's vale, or abounding in wealth,
At home and abroad, on the land, on the sea —
The Lord, the Almighty, thy strength
    e'er shall be.   *L. H., 427:2.*

*120. "Fear not, I am with thee; oh, be not dismayed;
For I am thy God and will still give thee aid;
I'll strengthen thee, help thee, and cause thee
    to stand,
Upheld by My righteous, omnipotent hand.
                        L. H., 427:3.

"When through the deep waters I call thee
    to go,
The rivers of sorrow shall not overflow;
For I will be with thee thy troubles to bless
And sanctify to thee thy deepest distress."
                        L. H., 427:4.

121. *Review Lessons 119, 120.*

122. *Review Lessons 109–112.*

123. *Review Lessons 114–117.*

124. *Review Lessons 119, 120.*

125. *Review Lessons 109–120.*

Unit XVI — Sin and Punishment

126. *Review Grade III, Lessons 122–126; Grade IV, Lessons 122–126.*

127. *Review Grade V, Lessons 117–121.*

128. We are born sinful.

    220. The imagination of man's heart. . . . *Gen. 8:21.*

    Sin proceeds from an evil heart.

    134. Out of the heart proceed. . . . *Matt. 15:19.*

129. God warns against hypocrisy.

    91. This people draweth nigh. . . . *Matt. 15:8.*

    To break the marriage ties is sin.

    142. What therefore God hath joined. . . . *Matt. 19:6.*

    *Corrupt speech is sin.

    151. Let no corrupt communication. . . . *Eph. 4:29.*

130. *Review Lessons 128, 129.*

Unit XVII — Forgiveness of Sins

131. *Review Grade IV, Lessons 129–133.*

132. *Review Grade V, Lessons 125–127.*

132. *Review Grade V, Lessons 125–129.* God forgives sins.

    488. Who shall lay anything to the charge. . . . *Rom. 8:33.*

Unit XVIII — The Passion

134. *Review Grade III, Lessons 130–133.*

Unit XIX — Easter: The Resurrection

135. *Review Grade III, Lessons 135–137;*
Grade IV, Lesson 136.

136. *Review Grade V, Lessons 134–137.*

137. All shall arise on Judgment Day.

 510. They shall come forth. . . . *John 5:29.*

Unit XX — The Sacraments

138. *Review Grade V, Lesson 108.*
The Lord's Supper is not for unbelievers.

 674. Ye cannot be partakers. . . . *1 Cor. 10:21.*

 681. Whosoever shall eat this bread. . . .
  1 Cor. 11:27.

Unit XXI — Death and Heaven

139. *Review Grade IV, Lesson 117;*
Grade V, Lessons 139–141.

140. We must remain faithful until the end.

 703. Hold that fast. . . . *Rev. 3:11.*

Christians are sure of eternal life.

 333. The Lord shall deliver me. . . .
  2 Tim. 4:18.

141. 528. My sheep hear My voice. . . .
  John 10:27, 28.

142. 522. I reckon that the sufferings. . . . *Rom. 8:18.*

 *518. Blessed are the dead. . . . *Rev. 14:13.*

143. *Review Lessons 140–142.*

144. Prayer for Faithfulness to the End.
   Let me be Thine forever,
      Thou faithful God and Lord;
   Let me forsake Thee never
      Nor wander from Thy Word;
   Lord, do not let me waver,
      But give me steadfastness,
   And for such grace forever
      Thy holy name I'll bless.   *L. H., 334:1.*

145. Lord Jesus, my Salvation,
      My Light, my Life divine,
   My only Consolation,
      Oh, make me wholly Thine!
   For Thou hast dearly bought me
      With blood and bitter pain.
   Let me, since Thou hast sought me,
      Eternal life obtain.   *L. H., 334:2.*

146. And Thou, O Holy Spirit,
      My Comforter and Guide,
   Grant that in Jesus' merit
      I always may confide,
   Him to the end confessing
      Whom I have known by faith.
   Give me Thy constant blessing
      And grant a Christian death. *L. H., 334:3.*

147. *Review Lessons 144–146.*

148. *Review Lessons 140–146.*

Unit XXII — Christian Living

149. Believers must perform good works.

444. He that abideth in Me. . . . *John 15:5.*

564. Let your light so shine. . . . *Matt. 5:16.*

*442. We are His workmanship. . . . *Eph. 2:10.*

*150. Christians are freed from the Ceremonial Law of the Old Testament.

98. Let no man therefore judge you. . . .
Col. 2:16, 17.

151. Christians must not give offense.

627. Whoso shall offend one. . . . *Matt. 18:6.*
God strengthens His children in temptation.
606. God is faithful. . . . *1 Cor. 10:13.*

152. *Review Lessons 149–151.*

Unit XXIII — The Judgment

153. *Review Grade IV, Lesson 118;*
Grade V, Lesson 107.

154. Damnation is eternal.

514. Their worm shall not die. . . . *Is. 66:24.*

Unit XXIV — Review

155. *Review Lessons 3–5.*

156. *Review Lessons 10, 11, 18.*

157. *Review Lessons 19–21.*

158. *Review Lessons 23, 24.*

159. *Review Lessons 29–31.*

160. *Review Lessons 58–60.*

161. *Review Lessons 62, 63.*

162. *Review Lessons 72–74.*

163. *Review Lessons 78, 79.*

164. *Review Lessons 82, 83.*

165. *Review Lessons 128, 129.*

Unit XXV — The Ascension

166. *Review Grade IV, Lessons 166–169.*

Unit XXVI — Pentecost; Mission Work

167. *Review Grade III, Lessons 169–173. Grade V, Lesson 172.*

Unit XXVII — Review

168. *Review Lessons 94, 95.*

169. *Review Lessons 96, 97.*

170. *Review Lessons 94–97.*

171. *Review Lessons 99–101.*

172. *Review Lessons 99–102.*

173. *Review Lessons 106, 109.*

174. *Review Lessons 110–112.*

175. *Review Lessons 114–117.*

176. *Review Lessons 119, 120.*

177. *Review Lessons 133, 137, 138, 154.*

178. *Review Lessons 140–142.*

179. *Review Lessons 144–146.*

180. *Review Lessons 149–151.*

Grade 7

Unit I — God

1. *Review Grade IV, Lessons 3–8.*

2. *Review Grade V, Lessons 4, 5; Grade VI, Lesson 3.*

3. *Review Grade VI, Lessons 4, 6.*

4. God is eternal.

   29. Lord, Thou hast been our Dwelling Place. . . . *Ps. 90:1, 2.*

   God created heaven and earth.

   416. By the word of the Lord. . . . *Ps. 33:6.*

Unit II — God's Word

5. *Review Grade IV, Lessons 28, 29; Grade V, Lessons 9–11.*

6. *Review Grade VI, Lessons 10, 11.*

7. We are brought to faith through the Gospel.

   19. I am not ashamed of the Gospel. . . . *Rom. 1:16.*

   Man dare not change God's Word.

   90. What thing soever I command you. . . . *Deut. 12:32.*

   God demands diligent use of His Word.

   111. This Book of the Law. . . . *Josh. 1:8.*

8. *Review Lessons 4, 7.*

135

Unit III — Review of Selections Memorized in Grade I

9. *Review Lessons 1, 2, 4, 6–10, 14–21, 24, 25, 27, 28.*

10. *Review Lessons 54–56, 59, 61–63, 65–68, 70–73.*

11. *Review Lessons 77, 78, 80, 81, 99–102, 104, 105, 107, 108, 110–115.*

12. *Review Lessons 123, 124, 127, 128, 130, 131, 133–138.*

Unit IV — Prayer

13. *Review Grade IV, Lessons 17–24, 99–101.*

14. *Review Grade IV, Lessons 103–110.*

15. *Review Grade V, Lessons 19–23.*

16. *Review Grade V, Lessons 19–27.*

17. *Review Grade VI, Lessons 18–21.*

18. *Review Grade VI, Lessons 23, 24.*

19. We should take all our needs to God in prayer.
    538. Be careful for nothing. . . . *Phil. 4:6.*

    Only God, not the saints, can hear prayer.
    535. Doubtless Thou art our Father. . . .
    Is. 63:16.

20. Prayer before Meals.
    Lord Jesus Christ, be Thou our Guest,
    Our morning Joy, our evening Rest,
    And with our daily bread impart
    Thy love and peace to every heart.
    A. C. S., 55.

Prayer after Meals.

As Thou, O Lord, art good and kind
　And gracious and forgiving,
Let us receive our daily bread
　With meekness and thanksgiving.

21. *Review Lessons 19, 20.*

22. An Evening Hymn.

Abide with me! Fast falls the eventide;
The darkness deepens; Lord, with me abide.
When other helpers fail and comforts flee,
Help of the helpless, oh, abide with me!

L. H., 552:1.

Swift to its close ebbs out life's little day;
Earth's joys grow dim, its glories pass away;
Change and decay in all around I see.
O Thou, who changest not, abide with me!

L. H., 552:2.

23. I need Thy presence every passing hour;
What but Thy grace can foil the Tempter's
　power?
Who like Thyself my guide and stay can be?
Through cloud and sunshine, oh, abide
　with me!　　*L. H., 552:6.*

*I fear no foe, with Thee at hand to bless;
Ills have no weight and tears no bitterness.
Where is death's sting? where, grave, thy
　victory?
I triumph still if Thou abide with me.

L. H., 552:7.

Hold Thou Thy cross before my closing eyes,
Shine through the gloom, and point me to
the skies.
Heaven's morning breaks, and earth's vain
shadows flee;
In life, in death, O Lord, abide with me!

L. H., 552:8.

24. *Review Lessons 22, 23.*

*25. Praise and Thanksgiving Hymn.

Come, ye thankful people, come;
Raise the song of Harvest Home.
All be safely gathered in
Ere the winter storms begin;
God, our Maker, doth provide
For our wants to be supplied.
Come to God's own temple, come;
Raise the song of Harvest Home.

L. H., 574:1

All the world is God's own field,
Fruit unto His praise to yield;
Wheat and tares together sown,
Unto joy or sorrow grown,
First the blade and then the ear,
Then the full corn shall appear.
Lord of harvest, grant that we
Wholesome grain and pure may be.

L. H., 574:2.

*26. For the Lord, our God, shall come
And shall take His harvest home;
From His field shall in that day
All offenses purge away;

Give His angels charge at last
In the fire the tares to cast,
But the fruitful ears to store
In His garner evermore.   *L. H., 574:3.*

Even so, Lord, quickly come
To Thy final Harvest Home;
Gather Thou Thy people in,
Free from sorrow, free from sin,
There, forever purified,
In Thy garner to abide.
Come with all Thine angels, come,
Raise the glorious Harvest Home.

                                   L. H., 574:4.
27. *Review Lessons 25, 26.*

28. Song of Praise.

Praise to the Lord, the Almighty, the King
    of creation!
O my soul, praise Him, for He is thy Health
    and Salvation!
Join the full throng;
Wake, harp and psalter and song;
Sound forth in glad adoration!   *L. H., 39:1.*

Praise to the Lord, who o'er all things so
    wondrously reigneth,
Who as on wings of an eagle, uplifteth,
    sustaineth.
Hast thou not seen
How thy desires all have been
Granted in what He ordaineth?   *L. H., 39:2.*

Praise to the Lord, who hath fearfully,
   wondrously made thee;
Health hath vouchsafed and, when heedlessly
   falling, hath stayed thee.
What need or grief
Ever hath failed of relief?
Wings of His mercy did shade thee.

L. H., 39:3.

29. Praise to the Lord, who doth prosper thy work
   and defend thee,
Who from the heavens the streams of His
   mercy doth send thee.
Ponder anew
What the Almighty can do,
Who with His love doth befriend thee.

L. H., 39:4.

Praise to the Lord! Oh, let all that is in me
   adore Him!
All that hath life and breath, come now with
   praises before Him!
Let the Amen
Sound from His people again;
Gladly for aye we adore Him.   *L. H., 39:5.*

30. *Review Lessons 28, 29.*

31. *Review Lessons 19, 20.*

32. *Review Lessons 22, 23.*

33. *Review Lessons 25, 26.*

34. *Review Lessons 28, 29.*

Unit V — The Reformation

35. *Review Grade V, Lessons 30–34.*

36. A Reformation Hymn.

> Lord, keep us steadfast in Thy Word;
> Curb those who fain by craft and sword
> Would wrest the Kingdom from Thy Son
> And set at naught all He hath done.
>
> *L. H., 261:1.*

> Lord Jesus Christ, Thy power make known,
> For Thou art Lord of lords alone;
> Defend Thy Christendom that we
> May evermore sing praise to Thee.
>
> *L. H., 261:2.*

> O Comforter of priceless worth,
> Send peace and unity on earth.
> Support us in our final strife
> And lead us out of death to life.
>
> *L. H., 261:3.*

Unit VI — Catechism Review

First Chief Part.

37. *Commandments 1–4.*

38. *Commandments 5–8.*

39. *Commandment 9 to Close of Commandments.*

40. *Entire First Chief Part.*

Second Chief Part.

41. *First and Second Article.*

42. *Entire Second Chief Part.*

Third Chief Part.

43. *Introduction to Second Petition.*

44. *Third to Fifth Petition.*

45. *Sixth Petition to Conclusion.*

46. *Entire Third Chief Part.*

Fourth Chief Part.

47. *Baptism, first five questions.*

48. *Baptism, last two questions.*

49. *Entire Fourth Chief Part.*

Unit VII — Salvation and Faith

50. *Review Grade IV, Lessons 53–59.*

51. *Review Grade V, Lessons 55–59.*

52. *Review Grade VI, Lessons 58–60.*

53. *Review Grade VI, Lessons 62, 63.*

54. Christ wants us to be saved.

   521. Father, I will that they also. . . .
      John 17:24.

   Faith in Christ saves.

   525. He that believeth on the Son. . . .
      John 3:36.

55. We have eternal life in Christ.

   17. In this was manifested the love of God. . . .
      1 John 4:9.

   486. God was in Christ. . . . *2 Cor. 5:19.*

56. We can and must be sure of our salvation.

   499. I am persuaded that neither death. . . .
      Rom. 8:38, 39.

57. *Review Lessons 54–56.*

Unit VIII — Catechism Review

Fifth Chief Part.

58. *Office of the Keys, three questions.*

59. *Confession, three questions.*

60. *Entire Fifth Chief Part.*

Sixth Chief Part.

61. *Sacrament of the Altar, first three questions.*

62. *Sacrament of the Altar, last two questions.*

63. *Entire Sixth Chief Part.*

64. Table of Duties.
    What the Hearers Owe to their Pastors, first four paragraphs.

65. What the Hearers Owe to their Pastors, last two paragraphs.

66. What the Hearers Owe to Their Pastors.

67. Of Civil Government, first three sentences.
    To Husbands.

68. To Wives; To Parents; To Children; To All in Common.

Unit IX — Christmas and New Year

69. *Review Grade IV, Lessons 69–71; Grade V, Lessons 73, 74.*

70. *Review Grade VI, Lessons 72–74.*

71. Christ became man.
    [307.] The Word was made flesh. . . . *John 1:14.*

    A Christmas Hymn.
    Let the earth now praise the Lord,
    Who hath truly kept His word
    And the sinners' Help and Friend
    Now at last to us doth send.   *L. H., 91:1.*

    What the fathers most desired,
    What the prophets' heart inspired,
    What they longed for many a year,
    Stands fulfilled in glory here.   *L. H., 91:2.*

72. Abram's promised great Reward,
Zion's Helper, Jacob's Lord —
Him of twofold race behold —
Truly came, as long foretold.   *L. H., 91:3.*

Welcome, O my Savior, now!
Hail! My Portion, Lord, art Thou.
Here, too, in my heart, I pray,
Oh, prepare Thyself a way!   *L. H., 91:4.*

73. *Review Lessons 71, 72.*

74. New Year's Prayer.

Help us, O Lord! Behold, we enter
   Upon another year today;
In Thee our hopes and thoughts now center,
   Renew our courage for the way.
New life, new strength, new happiness,
We ask of Thee — oh, hear and bless!
            L. H., 120:1.

May every plan and undertaking
   This year be all begun with Thee;
When I am sleeping or am waking,
   Still let me know Thou art with me.
Abroad do Thou my footsteps guide,
At home be ever at my side.   *L. H., 120:2.*

75. *Review Lessons 71—74.*

Unit X — Love

76. *Review Grade IV, Lessons 75, 76;*
Grade V, Lessons 78—81.

77. *Review Grade VI, Lessons 78, 79.*

Unit XI — Trust.

78. *Review Grade IV, Lessons 78, 79.*

79. *Review Grade VI, Lessons 82, 83.*

80. Complete trust in God is necessary.
>   60. Trust in the Lord with all thine heart. . . .
>   *Prov. 3:5.*

>   *We should not trust in riches.
>   62. How hard is it for them. . . . *Mark 10:24.*
>   God blesses our troubles.
>   274. Ye thought evil against me. . . . *Gen. 50:20.*

81. A Song of Trust.
>   All depends on our possessing
>   God's abundant grace and blessing,
>   Though all earthly wealth depart.
>   He who trusts with faith unshaken
>   In his God is not forsaken
>   And e'er keeps a dauntless heart.
>   *L. H., 425:1.*

>   He who hitherto hath fed me
>   And to many joys hath led me
>   Is and ever shall be mine.
>   He who did so gently school me,
>   He who still doth guide and rule me,
>   Will remain my Help divine. *L. H., 425:2.*

82. Many spend their lives in fretting
>   Over trifles and in getting
>   Things that have no solid ground.
>   I shall strive to win a treasure
>   That will bring me lasting pleasure
>   And that now is seldom found.
>   *L. H., 425:3.*

Well He knows what best to grant me;
All the longing hopes that haunt me,
   Joy and sorrow, have their day.
I shall doubt His wisdom never –
As God wills, so be it ever, –
   I to Him commit my way.   *L. H., 425:5.*

83. *Review Lessons 81, 82.*

84 *Review Lessons 80–82.*

Unit XII — Catechism

85. Table of Duties. To the Young in General.

86. Christian Questions, 1–7.

87. Christian Questions, 8–10.

88. Christian Questions, 11, 12.

89. *Review Lessons 86–88.*

90. *Review Lessons 85–88.*

Unit XIII — Review of Selections Memorized in Grade II

91. *Review Lessons 2–6, 16–18, 20, 21, 24–27.*

92. *Review Lessons 29–31, 35, 36, 51–53, 55, 56, 70–72.*

93. *Review Lessons 75, 76, 78–84, 96, 97, 99, 100.*

94. *Review Lessons 102, 103, 105, 107, 108, 110, 111, 113, 114.*

95. *Review Lessons 123–126, 128–130, 135–137, 169, 172.*

Unit XIV — Obedience

96. *Review Grade IV, Lesson 116;*
Grade V, Lessons 167–169.

97. *Review Grade VI, Lessons 29–31.*

98. We must obey the government.

120. Whosoever therefore resisteth the power. . . . *Rom. 13:2.*

Unit XV — The Judgment

99. *Review Grade IV, Lesson 118;*
Grade V, Lesson 107; Grade VI, Lesson 154.

100. All people will be judged by Christ.

396. We must all appear. . . . *2 Cor. 5:10.*

101. Judgment Day will come unexpectedly.

401. The Day of the Lord will come. . . .
2 Peter 3:10.

*402. As the lightning cometh. . . . *Matt. 24:27.*

Unit XVI — Death and Heaven

102. *Review Grade IV, Lesson 117;*
Grade V, Lessons 139–141.

103. *Review Grade VI, Lessons 140–142.*

104. *Review Grade VI, Lessons 144–146.*

*105. The Christian does not fear death.

357. O death, where is thy sting? . . .
1 Cor. 15:55-57.

Unit XVII — The Sacraments

106. *Review Grade V, Lesson 108;*
Grade VI, Lessons 106, 138.

107. Only believers have the benefit of the Lord's Supper.

684. As often as ye eat this bread. . . .
1 Cor. 11:26-28.

108. *Review Lessons 100, 101, 105, 107.*

Unit XVIII — Cross and Comfort

109. *Review Grade V, Lessons 109–113.*

110. *Review Grade VI, Lessons 109–112.*

111. *Review Grade VI, Lessons 114–117.*

112. *Review Grade VI, Lessons 119, 120.*

113, 114. A Hymn of Comfort.

In God, my faithful God,
I trust when dark my road;
Though many woes o'ertake me,
Yet He will not forsake me.
His love it is doth send them
And, when 'tis best, will end them.

L. H., 526:1.

My sins assail me sore,
But I despair no more.
I build on Christ, who loves me;
From this Rock nothing moves me.
To Him I all surrender,
To Him, my soul's Defender.

L. H., 526:2.

If death my portion be,
Then death is gain to me
And Christ my Life forever,
From whom death cannot sever.
Come when it may, He'll shield me,
To Him I wholly yield me.

L. H., 526:3.

Unit XIX — Sin and Punishment

115. *Review Grade IV, Lessons 122–126.*

116. *Review Grade V, Lessons 117–121.*

117. *Review Grade VI, Lessons 128, 129.*

118. The use of corrupt language is sin.
     79. With the tongue bless we God. . . .
         James 3:9, 10.

119. Revenge is sin.
     131. Dearly beloved, avenge not yourselves. . . .
         Rom. 12:19.
     To break the marriage ties is sin.
     143. Whosoever shall put away his wife. . . .
         Matt. 19:9.

120. *Review Lessons 118, 119.*

Unit XX — Forgiveness of Sins

121. *Review Grade IV, Lessons 129–133.*

122. *Review Grade V, Lessons 125–127.*

123. *Review Grade V, Lessons 125–129;
     Grade VI, Lesson 133.*

124. We are not worthy of God's mercy.
     278. I am not worthy. . . . *Gen. 32:10.*
     *Christ saved us from our sins.
     330. If any man sin. . . . *1 John 2:1, 2.*

125. Christ saved us from our sins.
     366. Surely He hath borne our griefs. . . .
         Is. 53:4, 5.

126. We must confess our guilt.
     665. If we say that we have no sin. . . .
         1 John 1:8, 9.
     *God forgives the sins of the penitent.
     653. The sacrifices of God. . . . *Ps. 51:17.*

127. Christ's sacrifice for our sins is complete.
     687. By one offering He hath perfected. . .
         Heb. 10:14, 18.

128. *Review Lessons 124–127.*

Unit XXI — The Passion

129. Christ is our Mediator.

> 304. There is one God. . . . *1 Tim. 2:5.*

> Christ came to destroy the works of the devil.

> 360. For this purpose the Son of God was
> manifested. . . . *1 John 3:8.*

130. Passion Hymn.

> Jesus, I will ponder now
>   On Thy holy Passion;
> With Thy Spirit me endow
>   For such meditation.
> Grant that I in love and faith
>   May the image cherish
> Of Thy suffering, pain, and death
>   That I may not perish.   *L. H., 140:1.*

131. Grant that I may willingly
>   Bear with Thee my crosses,
> Learning humbleness of Thee,
>   Peace mid pain and losses.
> May I give Thee love for love!
>   Hear me, O my Savior,
> That I may in heaven above
>   Sing Thy praise forever.   *L. H., 140:6.*

132. *Review Lessons 129–131.*

Unit XXII — Easter: The Resurrection

133. *Review Grade IV, Lesson 136;*
>   *Grade V, Lesson 134; Grade VI, Lesson 137.*

134. *Review Grade V, Lessons 134–137.*

135. We shall rise to eternal life.
     507. I know that my Redeemer liveth. . . .
          Job 19:25-27.

136. Easter Hymn.
     Awake, my heart, with gladness,
       See what today is done;
     Now, after gloom and sadness,
       Comes forth the glorious Sun.
     My Savior there was laid
     Where our bed must be made
     When to the realms of light
     Our spirit wings its flight.   *L. H., 192:1.*

137. The Foe in triumph shouted
       When Christ lay in the tomb;
     But, lo, he now is routed,
       His boast is turned to gloom.
     For Christ again is free;
     In glorious victory
     He who is strong to save
     Has triumphed o'er the grave.   *L. H., 192:2.*

138. This is a sight that gladdens;
       What peace it doth impart!
     Now nothing ever saddens
       The joy within my heart.
     No gloom shall ever shake,
     No foe shall ever take,
     The hope which God's own Son
     In love for me hath won.   *L. H., 192:3.*

139. *Review Lessons 135–138.*

Unit XXIII — Christian Living

140. *Review Grade VI, Lessons 149, 150.*

141. *Review Grade VI, Lessons 149–151.*

142. Love of the world separates from God.
    578. Love not the world. . . . *1 John 2:15-17.*

143. We must not serve self, but Christ.
    63. Whose God is their belly. . . . *Phil. 3:19.*
    693. He died for all. . . . *2 Cor. 5:15, 17.*

144. *Review Lessons 142, 143.*

145. We must not defile our bodies with sin.
    157. Know ye not that your body. . . .
        1 Cor. 6:19.
    We must flee sin.
    156. Flee also youthful lusts. *2 Tim. 2:22.*
    The godly are blessed.
    198. Godliness is profitable. . . . *1 Tim. 4:8.*

146. The Christian has no reason to worry.
    591. Seek ye first the kingdom of God. . . .
        Matt. 6:33, 34.

147. *Review Lessons 142–146.*

148. We should begin and end our work in Christ.
    With the Lord begin thy task,
        Jesus will direct it;
    For His aid and counsel ask,
        Jesus will perfect it.
    Every morn with Jesus rise,
        And when day is ended,
    In His name then close thine eyes;
        Be to Him commended.   *L. H., 540:1.*

149. Let each day begin with prayer,
    Praise and adoration;
On the Lord cast every care,
    He is thy Salvation.
Morning, evening, and at night
    Jesus will be near thee,
Save thee from the Tempter's might,
    With His presence cheer thee.   *L. H., 540:2.*

150. With thy Savior at thy side,
    Foes need not alarm thee;
In His promises confide,
    And no ill can harm thee.
All thy trust do thou repose
    In the mighty Master,
Who in wisdom truly knows
    How to stem disaster.   *L. H., 540:3.*

151. *Review Lessons 148–150.*

152. *Review Lessons 142–150.*

Unit XXIV — Review

153. *Review Lessons 4, 7.*

154. *Review Lessons 19, 20.*

155. *Review Lessons 22, 23.*

156. *Review Lessons 25, 26.*

157. *Review Lessons 28, 29.*

158. *Review Lessons 54–56.*

159. *Review Lessons 71–74.*

160. *Review Lessons 80–82.*

161. *Review Lessons 85–87.*

162. *Review Lessons 85–88.*

163. *Review Lessons 98, 100, 101, 105.*

164. *Review Lessons 107, 113, 114.*

165. *Review Lessons 36, 118, 119.*

Unit XXV — The Ascension

166. *Review Grade IV, Lessons 166–169.*

Unit XXVI — Pentecost; Mission Work

167. *Review Grade V, Lesson 172.*
    *The Holy Ghost works faith in us.
    428. Ye are a chosen generation. . . .
       1 Peter 2:9.

168. Pentecost Hymn.

   O Holy Spirit, enter in
   And in our hearts Thy work begin,
     Thy temple deign to make us;
   Sun of the soul, Thou Light Divine,
   Around and in us brightly shine,
     To joy and gladness wake us
   That we, In Thee
   Truly living, To Thee giving
   Prayer unceasing,
   May in love be still increasing.   *L. H., 235:1.*

169. Give to Thy Word impressive power
  That in our hearts, from this good hour,
    As fire it may be glowing;
  That we confess the Father, Son,
  And Thee, the Spirit, Three in One,
    Thy glory ever showing.
  Stay Thou, Guide now
  Our souls ever That they never
  May forsake Thee,
  But by faith their Refuge make Thee.

L. H., 235:2

170. *Review Lessons 167–169.*

171. We must preach God's Word in truth.
  472. He that hath My Word. . . . *Jer. 23:28.*
  The Church has power to forgive and retain sins.
  646. Verily I say unto you. . . . *Matt. 18:18.*

172. Christians must support the Church cheerfully.
  114. Let him that is taught. . . . *Gal. 6:6, 7.*
  The invisible Church will remain until Judgment Day.
  463. Thou art Peter. . . . *Matt. 16:18.*

173. *Review Lessons 167–172.*

Unit XXVII — Review

174. *Review Lessons 124–127.*

175. *Review Lessons 129–131.*

176. *Review Lessons 135–138.*

177. *Review Lessons 142–146.*

178. *Review Lessons 148–150.*

179. *Review Lessons 167–169.*

180. *Review Lessons 171, 172.*

MEMORY SELECTIONS

Grade 8

Unit I — God

LESSONS

1. *Review Grade V, Lessons 4, 5; Grade VI, Lesson 3.*

2. *Review Grade VI, Lessons 4, 6; Grade VII, Lesson 4.*

3. God knows everything.

    35. O Lord, Thou hast searched me. . . . *Ps. 139:1-4.*

4. It is foolish to deny God.

    64. The fool hath said in his heart. . . . *Ps. 14:1.*

    *Christ is our exalted Lord.

    373. God also hath highly exalted Him. . . . *Phil. 2:9-11.*

5. *Review Lessons 3, 4.*

Unit II — God's Word

6. *Review Grade V, Lessons 9–11.*

7. *Review Grade VI, Lessons 10, 11; Grade VII, Lesson 7.*

8. The benefits of God's Word are great.

    8. From a child thou hast known. . . . *2 Tim. 3:15-17.*

9. God's Word should be used reverently.

   107. Keep thy foot when thou goest. . . .
        Eccl. 5:1.

   God's Word always bears fruit.

   470. As the rain cometh down. . . . *Is. 55:10, 11.*

10. Christians love the house of God. . . .

    108. Lord, I have loved the habitation. . . .
         Ps. 26:8.

    *We should beware of false prophets.

    482. Now, I beseech you, brethren. . . .
         Rom. 16:17.

11. *Review Lessons 8–10.*

Unit III — Prayer

12. *Review Grade V, Lessons 19–23.*

13. *Review Grade V, Lessons 19–27.*

14. *Review Grade VI, Lessons 18–21.*

15. *Review Grade VI, Lessons 23, 24.*

16. *Review Grade VII, Lessons 19–23.*

17. *Review Grade VII, Lessons 25, 26.*

18. *Review Grade VII, Lessons 28, 29.*

19. Prayer must come from the heart.

    529. Let the words of my mouth. . . . *Ps. 19:14.*
    *Prayer must flow from faith.

    549. Let him ask in faith. . . . *James 1:6, 7.*

20. Prayer before Meals.
Feed Thy children, God most holy,
Comfort sinners poor and lowly;
O Thou Bread of life from heaven,
Bless the food Thou here hast given!
As these gifts the body nourish,
May our souls in graces flourish
Till with saints in heavenly splendor
At Thy feast due thanks we render.

21. Psalm of Praise.   *L. H., 659.*
Psalm 100:1-3.

22. Psalm 100:4, 5.

23. *Review Lessons 19–22.*

Unit IV — Review of Selections Memorized in Grade III

24. *Review Lessons 3, 4, 6, 7, 17–21, 23, 24.*

25. *Review Lessons 25–27, 32, 33, 35–37, 54–57, 59, 60.*

26. *Review Lessons 62, 63, 69–72, 76–79, 83, 84.*

27. *Review Lessons 119, 122–126, 130–133, 135–137.*

28. *Review Lessons 140–145, 169–173.*

Unit V — Review of Selections Memorized in Grade IV

29. *Review Lessons 3, 4, 6–8, 17, 18, 20–24.*

30. *Review Lessons 28, 29, 53–55, 57–59, 69.*

31. *Review Lessons 70, 71, 75, 76, 78, 79, 99–101.*

32. *Review Lessons 103, 104, 106–108, 110, 116–118, 122, 123.*

33. *Review Lessons 125, 126, 129–131, 133, 136, 166–169.*

Unit V (a) — The Reformation

34. *Review Grade V, Lessons 30–34.*
35. *Review Grade VII, Lesson 36.*

Unit VI — Catechism Review

First Chief Part.
36. *Commandments 1–6.*
37. *Commandment 7 to Close of Commandments.*
38. *Entire First Chief Part.*
    Second Chief Part.
39. *First and Second Articles.*
40. *Entire Second Chief Part.*
    Third Chief Part.
41. *Introduction to Second Petition.*
42. *Third to Fifth Petitions.*
43. *Sixth Petition to Conclusion.*
44. *Entire Third Chief Part.*
    Fourth Chief Part.
45. *Baptism, first five questions.*
46. *Baptism, last two questions.*
47. *Entire Fourth Chief Part.*
    Fifth Chief Part.
48. *Office of the Keys, three questions.*
49. *Confession, three questions.*
50. *Entire Fifth Chief Part.*
    Sixth Chief Part.
51. *Sacrament of the Altar, first three questions.*
52. *Sacrament of the Altar, last two questions.*
53. *Entire Sixth Chief Part.*

Unit VII — Salvation and Faith

54. *Review Grade V, Lessons 55–59.*

55. *Review Grade VI, Lessons 58–60.*

56. *Review Grade VI, Lessons 62, 63.*

57. *Review Grade VII, Lessons 54–56.*

58. We are reconciled to God through Christ.
   233. Christ hath redeemed us. . . . *Gal. 3:13.*
   493. God was in Christ. . . . *2 Cor. 5:19.*

59. We are saved by grace.
   426. God hath saved us. . . . *2 Tim. 1:9.*
   *490. There is no difference. . . . *Rom. 3:22-24.*

60. *Review Lessons 58, 59.*

61. Faith must be a matter of the heart.
   239. Thou believest that there is one God. . . .
      James 2:19.

   The unbeliever has no spiritual understanding.
   222. The natural man receiveth not. . . .
      1 Cor. 2:14.

62. Only the believers can see the works of God.
   246. Through faith we understand. . . .
      Heb. 11:3.

   The unbeliever is an enemy of God.
   224. The carnal mind is enmity. . . . *Rom. 8:7.*
   God does not reject a weak faith.
   695. A bruised reed shall He not break. . . .
      Is. 42:3.

63. *Review Lessons 61, 62.*

64. *Review Lessons 58–62.*

Unit VIII — Catechism Review

65. Table of Duties.
    What the Hearers Owe to Their Pastors,
    first four paragraphs.

66. What the Hearers Owe to Their Pastors,
    complete.

67. Of Civil Government, first three sentences;
    To Husbands; To Wives.

68. To Parents; To Children; To the Young in
    General; To All in Common.

Unit IX — Christmas and New Year

69. *Review Grade V, Lessons 73, 74.*

70. *Review Grade VI, Lessons 72–74.*

71. *Review Grade VII, Lessons 71, 72.*

72. *Review Grade VII, Lessons 71–74.*

73. Christ became man to redeem us.
    315. When the fullness of the time was come. . . .
        Gal. 4:4, 5.

Unit X — Love

74. *Review Grade V, Lessons 78–81.*

75. *Review Grade VI, Lessons 78, 79.*

Unit XI — Trust

76. *Review Grade VI, Lessons 82, 83.   Psalm 23.*

77. *Review Grade VII, Lessons 81, 82.*

78. *Review Grade VII, Lessons 80–82.*

79. A Psalm of Trust.
    Psalm 46:1-4.

80. Psalm 46:5-8.

81. Psalm 46:9-11.

82. *Review Lessons 79–81.   Psalm 46:1-11.*

83. A Psalm of Trust.
    Psalm 121:1-4.

84. Psalm 121:5-8

85. *Review Lessons 83, 84.   Psalm 121:1-8.*

86. *Review Lessons 79–84.   Psalms 46 and 121.*

Unit XII — Catechism

87. *Review Christian Questions, 1–9.*

88. *Review Christian Questions, 10–12.*

89. *Review Christian Questions, 1–12.*

90. Christian Questions, 13–15.

91. Christian Questions, 16, 17.

92. Christian Questions, 18, 19.

93. Christian Question, 20.

94. Christian Questions, 13–17.

95. Christian Questions, 18–20.

96. Christian Questions, 13–20.

Unit XIII — Obedience

97. *Review Grade V, Lessons 167–169;
    Grade VII, Lesson 98.*

98. *Review Grade VI, Lessons 29–31.*

99. God demands obedience to spiritual rulers.

   113. Obey them that have the rule. . . .
        Heb. 13:17.

   *Mere outward obedience is not enough.

   566. Thou that makest thy boast. . . .
        Rom. 2:23, 24.

Unit XIV — The Judgment

100. *Review Grade V, Lesson 107;*
     Grade VI, Lesson 154; Grade VII, Lessons 100, 101.

Unit XV — The Sacraments

101. *Review Grade V, Lesson 108;*
     Grade VI, Lessons 106, 138; Grade VII, Lesson 107.

102. We receive Christ's body and blood in the Lord's Supper.

   680. The cup of blessing. . . . *1 Cor. 10:16.*

   A Communion Hymn.

   Thy Table I approach,
     Dear Savior, hear my prayer;
   Oh, let no unrepented sin
     Prove hurtful to me there!   *L. H., 310:1.*

   Lo, I confess my sins
     And mourn their wretched bands;
   A contrite heart is sure to find
     Forgiveness at Thy hands.   *L. H., 310:2.*

103. Thy body and Thy blood,
       Once slain and shed for me,
     Are taken here with mouth and soul,
       In blest reality.   *L. H., 310:3.*

Search not how this takes place,
   This wondrous mystery;
God can accomplish vastly more
   Than seemeth plain to thee.   *L. H., 310:4.*

104. *Review Lessons 99, 102, 103.*

105. A Baptismal Hymn.

Baptized into Thy name most holy,
   O Father, Son, and Holy Ghost,
I claim a place, though weak and lowly,
   Among Thy seed, Thy chosen host.
Buried with Christ and dead to sin,
Thy Spirit now shall live within.   *L. H., 298:1.*

And I have vowed to fear and love Thee
   And to obey Thee, Lord, alone;
Because Thy Holy Ghost did move me,
   I dared to pledge myself Thine own,
Renouncing sin to keep the faith
And war with evil unto death.   *L. H., 298:3.*

106. *My faithful God, Thou failest never,
   Thy covenant surely will abide;
Oh, cast me not away forever
   Should I transgress it on my side!
Though I have oft my soul defiled,
Do Thou forgive, restore, Thy child.
                      L. H., 298:4.

And never let my purpose falter,
  O Father, Son, and Holy Ghost,
But keep me faithful to Thine altar
  Till Thou shalt call me from my post.
So unto Thee I live and die
And praise Thee evermore on high.

L. H., 298:6.

107. *Review Lessons 105, 106.*

108. *Review Lessons 102–106.*

Unit XVI — Cross and Comfort

109. *Review Grade V, Lessons 109–113.*

110. *Review Grade VI, Lessons 109–112.*

111. *Review Grade VI, Lessons 114–117.*

112. *Review Grade VI, Lessons 119, 120.*

113. *Review Grade VII, Lessons 113, 114.*

Unit XVII — Sin and Punishment

114. *Review Grade V, Lessons 117–121.*

115. *Review Grade VI, Lessons 128, 129;*
Grade VII, Lessons 118, 119.

116. Evil thoughts are sin.
  146. Whosoever looketh on a woman. . . .
    Matt. 5:28.

  We must flee sin.
  155. Flee fornication. *1 Cor. 6:18.*

117. Indecent thoughts, words, and deeds are forbidden.
  147. Fornication and all uncleanness. . . .
    Eph. 5:3, 4.

118. Each shall suffer for his own sin.
  197. The soul that sinneth. . . . *Ezek. 18:20.*

119. *Review Lessons 34–36.*

120. Love of money crowds out the love of God.
    187. Having food and raiment. . . .
        1 Tim. 6:8-10.

121. God punishes those who acquire wealth dishonestly.
    185. Woe unto them that join house. . . . *Is. 5:8.*

122. God condemns hypocrisy.
    186. Woe unto you, scribes. . . . *Matt. 23:14.*
    Even one sin condemns us.

    202. Whosoever shall keep the whole Law. . . .
        James 2:10.

123. *Review Lessons 38–40.*

124. *Review Lessons 34–40.*

Unit XVIII — Forgiveness of Sins

125. *Review Grade V, Lessons 125–127.*

126. *Review Grade V, Lessons 125–129;
    Grade VI, Lesson 133.*

127. *Review Grade VII, Lessons 124–127.*

128. Man's sins are great, but God's forgiveness is greater.
    485. If Thou, Lord, shouldest mark. . . .
        Ps. 130:3, 4.

    The church forgives and retains sins in God's name.

    651. If he shall neglect to hear them. . . .
        Matt. 18:17, 18, 20.

129. Those who do not forgive their fellow men have no forgiveness from God.

    598. When ye stand praying. . . . *Mark 11:25, 26.*

130. We must confess our sins.

   664. He that covereth his sins. . . . *Prov. 28:13.*

131. *Review Lessons 57–59.*

132. A Psalm of Forgiveness.
   Psalm 130:1-4.

133. Psalm 130:5-8.

134. *Review Lessons 132, 133. Psalm 130:1-8.*

135. *Review Lessons 128–133.*

Unit XIX — The Passion

136. *Review Grade VII, Lessons 129–131.*

Unit XX — Easter: The Resurrection

137. *Review Grade V, Lessons 134–137.*
   Grade VI, Lesson 137.

138. *Review Grade VII, Lessons 135–138.*

Unit XXI — Christian Living

139. *Review Grade VI, Lessons 149–151.*

140. *Review Grade VII, Lessons 142–145.*

141. *Review Grade VII, Lessons 146–150.*

°142. We are to be humble like Christ.

   334. Let this mind be in you. . . . *Phil. 2:5-8.*

143. The Christian must bear his cross.

   576. Then said Jesus unto His disciples. . . .
   Matt. 16:24.

   Powerful forces of evil make Christian life difficult.

   257. We wrestle not against flesh and blood. . . .
   Eph. 6:12.

144. *Review Lessons 142, 143.*

145. Hymn on Christian Family Life.

Oh, blest the house, whate'er befall,
Where Jesus Christ is all in all!
Yea, if He were not dwelling there,
How dark, and poor, and void it were!
                                    L. H., 625:1.

Oh, blest that house where faith ye find
And all within have set their mind
To trust their God and serve Him still
And do in all His holy will!   *L. H., 625:2.*

146. Oh, blest the parents who give heed
Unto their children's foremost need
And weary not of care or cost!
May none to them and heaven be lost!
                                    L. H., 625:3.

Blest such a house, it prospers well;
In peace and joy the parents dwell,
And in their children's lot is shown
How richly God can bless His own.
                                    L. H., 625:4.

Then here will I and mine today
A solemn covenant make and say:
Though all the world forsake Thy Word,
I and my house will serve the Lord.
                                    L. H., 625:5.

147. *Review Lessons 145, 146.*

*148. A Psalm on Christian Living.
Psalm 1:1-3.

*149. Psalm 1:4-6.

150. *Review Lessons 148, 149. Psalm 1:1-6.*

151. *Review Lessons 142–146.*

152. *Review Lessons 142–149.*

Unit XXII — Death and Heaven

153. *Review Grade V, Lessons 139–141.*
Grade VI, Lessons 140–142.

154. *Review Grade VI, Lessons 144–146;*
Grade VII, Lesson 105.

155, 156. Prayer for a Christian Death.

When my last hour is close at hand,
    Lord Jesus Christ, attend me;
Beside me then, O Savior, stand
    To comfort and defend me.
Into Thy hands I will commend
My soul at this my earthly end,
    And Thou wilt keep it safely.   L. H., 594:1.

My spirit I commend to Thee
    And gladly hence betake me;
Peaceful and calm my sleep shall be,
    No human voice can wake me.
But Christ is with me through the strife,
And He will bear me into life
    And open heaven before me.   L. H., 594:5.

Unit XXIII — Review

157. *Review Lessons 3, 4, 99.*

158. *Review Lessons 8–10.*

159. *Review Lessons 19–22.*

160. *Review Lessons 58, 59.*

161. *Review Lessons 61, 62, 73.*

162. *Review Lessons 79–81.*

163. *Review Lessons 83, 84.*

164. *Review Lessons 90, 91.*

165. *Review Lessons 92, 93.*

166. *Review Lessons 90–93.*

167. *Review Lessons 102, 103.*

168. *Review Lessons 105, 106.*

169. *Review Lessons 116–118.*

Unit XXIV — Pentecost; Mission Work

170. *Review Grade V, Lesson 172;*
Grade VII, Lessons 167–169.

171. *Review Grade VII, Lessons 167–172.*

172, 173. A Mission Hymn.

Hark! the voice of Jesus crying,
  "Who will go and work today?
Fields are white and harvests waiting,
  Who will bear the sheaves away?"
Loud and long the Master calleth,
  Rich reward He offers thee;
Who will answer, gladly saying,
  "Here am I, send me, send me?"

L. H., 496:1.

*If you cannot speak like angels,
   If you cannot preach like Paul,
You can tell the love of Jesus,
   You can say He died for all.
If you cannot rouse the wicked
   With the Judgment's dread alarms,
You can lead the little children
   To the Savior's waiting arms.   *L. H., 496:2.*

Let none hear you idly saying,
   "There is nothing I can do,"
While the souls of men are dying
   And the Master calls for you.
Take the task He gives you gladly,
   Let His work your pleasure be;
Answer quickly when He calleth,
   "Here am I, send me, send me!"   *L. H., 496:4.*

Unit XXV — Review